The Art of Being Alone

TANIKAWA SHUNTARŌ

The Art of Being Alone

POEMS 1952–2009

ଓଃ

TRANSLATED WITH AN INTRODUCTION

BY

TAKAKO U. LENTO

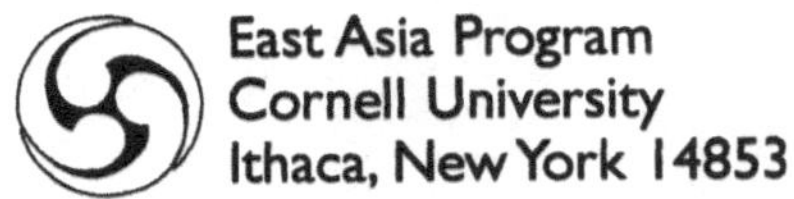

East Asia Program
Cornell University
Ithaca, New York 14853

The Cornell East Asia Series is published by the Cornell University East Asia Program (distinct from Cornell University Press). We publish reasonably priced books on a variety of scholarly topics relating to East Asia as a service to the academic community and the general public. Standing orders, which provide for automatic billing and shipping of each title in the series upon publication, are accepted.

If after review by internal and external readers a manuscript is accepted for publication, it is published on the basis of camera-ready copy provided by the volume author. Each author is thus responsible for any necessary copy editing and for manuscript formatting. Alternative arrangements should be made with approval of the Series. Address submission inquiries to CEAS Editorial Board, East Asia Program, Cornell University, Ithaca, New York 14853-7601.

Cover concept and book layout: Mai
Number 157 in the Cornell East Asia Series.
©2011 by Takako U. Lento. All rights reserved.
ISSN 1050-2955
ISBN 978-1-933947-27-3 hc
ISBN 978-1-933947-57-0 pb
Library of Congress Control Number: 2011926202

25 24 23 22 21 20 19 18 17 16 15 14 13 12 11   9 8 7 6 5 4 3 2 1

♾ The paper in this book meets the requirements for permanence of ISO 9706:1994.
CAUTION: Except for brief quotations in a review, no part of this book may be reproduced or utilized in any form, without the permission in writing from the editors. Please address inquiries to Takako U. Lento in care of East Asia Program, Cornell University, 140 Uris Hall, Ithaca, NY 14853-7601.

*This book follows Japanese
practice with respect to Japanese
names: family name (Tanikawa) first,
given name (Shuntarō) last.*

CONTENTS

Contents

Acknowledgment

First and foremost I am grateful to Mr. Tanikawa for his trust in me and his generosity in allowing the inclusion of a wide range of his poetry in this book. His responses to my questions have been always helpful, to the point, and limited to factual matters. I greatly appreciate his firm commitment to letting his poetry speak for itself and his willingness to allow alternate readings of the same poems.

Professor Martin Collcutt of Princeton University gave me practical guidance at the outset of this project. His suggestions set in motion the activities that led to this publication.

Professor Edwin Cranston of Harvard University played a critical part in the development of this book. Not only did he kindly read my preliminary essay and selected translations, he gave me insightful comments on Tanikawa the poet and his varied poetic style. It was at his suggestion that I approached the Cornell East Asia Series about publishing the book.

Mr. Yotsumoto Yasuhiro, poet and editor of PIW Japanese Domain, the online international poetry forum, offered encouraging comments on my translations and essays on Japanese poetry. His admiration of Mr. Tanikawa inspired me as I was working on this book.

W. S. Merwin gave me permission to include "Grass" and "Death and Flame 1940," which he translated based on my preliminary versions.

Mai Shaikhanuar-Cota, Managing Editor at CEAS, guided me through the comment and approval process. I owe her a debt of gratitude for her commitment to the publication of this book as part of the Series. She was supportive at every turn, and had an unwavering belief in the significance of Tanikawa's poetry.

Throughout all these activities, my husband Thomas Lento has been a wonderful cheerleader, a living encyclopedia, a cultural advisor, and an

English language specialist. As a published author himself, he helped me understand the process and taught me patience. His admiration of Tanikawa's poems made his advice all the more meaningful. I especially thank him for his patience in performing the final copy-editing of this book.

I would also like to evoke the spirit of the late Paul Engle, poet and teacher, who was "responsible for bringing Takako to the U.S," as he liked to put it, to participate in the University of Iowa Writers' Workshop and the pilot stage of the International Writing Program. All my literary activities since then have their roots in the opportunities he gave me.

Many others have been generous and kind to me, providing encouragement, advice, and support. I most sincerely thank them all.

Takako U. Lento

The Art of
Being Alone

INTRODUCTION

In the Beginning

In one corner of a large hall Tanikawa Shuntarō was sitting in a chair, legs crossed, all by himself. This was in early 1971 in New York, following a poetry reading by three prominent Japanese poets: Tanikawa, Tamura Ryūichi, and Katagiri Yuzuru. The excitement in the hall was still palpable, but he was like a bronze statue, back straight, head up. Earlier in the day I had finally met the poet whose work I had enjoyed reading since I was a teenager. I recall trying to connect the image of a poet I had imagined through reading his early work with the real person sitting there, seemingly in his own world.

Several days later, as part of a poetry-reading tour across the United States, all three poets were at the University of Iowa, in the heartland of America, on the eastern edge of the American West. Iowa's International Writing Program had invited them to stay for a few days and offer a poetry reading. During his stay Tanikawa had kindly agreed to visit my Modern Japanese Poetry class one afternoon to discuss poetry. The students were mostly from the University's Oriental Studies program. They were not only curious about the poet and his work, but also about his interest in their own American culture.

Tanikawa was personable, open, and responsive. His manner was quietly sophisticated with no pretensions. When he mentioned cowboy movies as one of the elements that influenced his work, a student asked him pointedly if he, as a Japanese, could really understand those Western movies, which embody the culture of the rugged old West and America's unique frontier spirit. At first Tanikawa seemed bemused by the question. The discussion ultimately led to a consideration of how a foreign culture or its products can influence a writer. The students seemed to accept his broad view that any subject can influence us according to the way each of us uniquely perceives or understands it, and that any real or imaginary borders that separate us from the subject matter are not relevant.

Much later I came upon Tanikawa's own account of what he took away from Western movies in his early years. He used his poem "Billy the Kid" (*On Love, 1955*) as an example.

For some period of time, the blue sky seemed to me to be an enemy that totally consumed me.

 . . . above me is my only enemy
 the dry blue sky. it has consumed me totally, while running, shooting, even making love, that blue sky has consumed me. but the only time it fails to consume me is when I die. now I will not be consumed. for the first time I have no fear of the blue sky. I am not afraid of that silence that fathomless blue.

— "Billy the Kid"

I believe [my attitude] is more conceptual, rather than emotional, but as you can see, I was looking at the then popular Western movies not as human drama, but as the drama of mankind against the Cosmos. What the gun-toting protagonist stood against was not his social order, but the vast and empty Cosmos. I considered the home life the American pioneers were trying to build as their fortress against a vast nothingness. I was trying to find the reference points of human survival against the vast and empty cosmos.

— *Kokubungaku* (*Japanese Literature*),
November 1995

On reading this passage I realized that while my students and I had understood in general terms the nature of influence as he discussed it, we did not really grasp what Tanikawa had in mind that day. In "Billy the Kid" he usurped a familiar theme of Western movies, so to speak, and elevated it to dramatize and personify his concept of human existence in the universe. No wonder his "Billy the Kid" moves us, and invites us to look at a deeper plane of humanity, from an angle totally different from Western movies. This ability to instantly and seamlessly convert mundane matters into a dramatized concept is what gives Tanikawa's poetry its magnetic quality. His poetry first captivates us with words and images that appear to be familiar and easy to understand, and then leads us into a world of its own. Since then I have been interested in going deeper into his poetry to see what I can find in that special world.

His Life and Work

Tanikawa Shuntarō was born in 1931 in Tokyo, the only child of intellectual and well-to-do parents. His father, Tanikawa Tetsuzō, was a distinguished philosopher, critic, and educator who later served as president of Hōsei University. He was particularly interested in the confluence of philosophy, literature, and the arts. Tanikawa's mother, Takiko, was a trained pianist with modern tastes. Growing up in a sophisticated and nurturing family atmosphere, he acquired his father's philosophical habit of mind and his mother's affection for the new and her love of music.

From his earliest childhood he and his family spent summers in their villa in the mountains of Kita-Karuizawa, northwest of Tokyo. As a youth, Tanikawa recalls, he would immerse himself in Nature there, contemplating his status as part of an orderly cosmos. This experience was to have a profound effect on his thought and writing.

In 1938 he entered elementary school in Tokyo. He was a bright student and a class leader. Outside of class he enjoyed building model planes and was fascinated by mechanical objects. This helps to explain his later interest in cutting-edge technology. In 1944 he advanced to middle school, also in Tokyo. By Tanikawa's own account, he felt so close to his mother that he experienced separation anxiety whenever they were apart, fearing he might lose her. This might have been because he was the only child of the family, but it may also have been an effect of growing up during the war and witnessing some of its horrors. He speaks of the time he and a playmate bicycled by "burned bodies like charred logs" the day after a bombing in Tokyo. In such an environment, it is not surprising that a sensitive young mind would be riddled with the fear of separation and death, and an awareness of the transience of life. According to Tanikawa himself, this happened even though his parents had carefully shielded him from the gruesome reality of war and its destructive power for much of his childhood.

In July 1945 Tanikawa and his mother took shelter from the Tokyo air raids at his grandfather's house in Kyoto. He attended a local school but felt isolated in the unfamiliar environment. After World War II ended he and his family went back to their home, which had been spared by the bombs. He returned to his old middle school in Tokyo in 1946. There he found that the pre-war and war-time totalitarian educational system had been totally revamped under Occupation guidelines, a change that must have been confusing to a child. Tanikawa later spoke of his shock and disbelief at the way his teachers abruptly negated the rigorous imperial discipline they had earlier tried to instill in children as absolute truth. He said, "The teachers lost all credibility with me to the extent that I lost interest in school altogether."

He turned instead to music, as he wrote in "To the World!" (1959):

Around the time I started middle school, I got to know music through Beethoven. And at the same time, something that transcends music. Probably because of that, I even thought I could be a servant to Beethoven himself, when his music conquered me. . . . Curiously, my deep emotional acceptance of his music led me to only one thought: "I can live." That was the only way I could verbalize my deep emotion.

Music has remained an important element of his life and work. He became a close friend of the late Takemitsu Tōru, an internationally renowned composer of modern music. Once an excellent, indeed, a model student, his disillusionment in and distrust of teachers and authority grew stronger. He completed his high school education in 1950 by switching to a night school program. He chose not to continue formal education beyond that.

Tanikawa had started writing poetry while in middle school, influenced by a poetry-minded classmate. He described his interest in poetry then as "toying with poetry as one would play Ping-Pong with one's friend," and he continued writing poetry through high school. He submitted poetry to magazines for students, often receiving awards and recognition. The poetry he kept writing in his notebooks turned out to be "helpful," as Tanikawa put it later, in launching his career as a poet.

Upon Tanikawa's declaration that he wanted to become a poet, his father consulted his friend Miyoshi Tatsuji, a renowned poet, and asked him to read some of the poems in his son's notebooks. Miyoshi was so impressed with them that he visited Tanikawa to congratulate him, and introduced him to the literary magazine *Bungaku-kai* (Literary World), which published "Nero and five poems" in 1950. In 1951 Tanikawa was named one of the notable poets by *Poetics*. In 1952 Sōgensha of Tokyo published his first book of poetry, *Alone in Two Billion Light Years*.

With this very first book Tanikawa was recognized as a poet among poets, and at the same time gained popularity among a large and diverse group of readers, old and young, educated and otherwise, with or without literary interests.

In 1953 he joined "Kai," a group of young poets, and later that year he published *62 Sonnets*. In 1955 he published his third book of poems, *On Love,* and wrote the first of over sixty radio dramas; radio was an important social medium at the time. Since then Tanikawa has published over sixty books of poetry of various types, including children's verses and nonsense poems, and had nearly twenty books of his selected poems edited by others.

One of Tanikawa's interests is linguistic experimentation. He has authored several books of rhythmic verses, including tongue-twisters and plays on words. In *Kotoba-asobi Uta* (Word-Play Verses) and its sequel, published in 1973 and 1981, respectively, he pushes the Japanese language to its limits, taking advantage of the cultural roots and nuances of words, and constructing sound patterns to create delightfully unusual poetic, phonetic, and metrical experiences for readers young and old.

These two books sold millions of copies in Japan. Unfortunately these fascinating and clever verses simply defy translation.

Tanikawa also authored picture books, children's stories, children's songs, school songs, and translations of children's books and poetry. His translations from English range from the plays of T. S. Eliot to *Mother Goose*. His Japanese translation of *Mother Goose* was awarded the Japan Translation Culture Award in 1975. In 1969 he became the official translator of "Peanuts," and made the American comic strip a popular favorite in Japan.

Tanikawa's other literary work includes a dozen books of essays, and more than fifteen volumes that reproduce his dialogues with Japanese experts and practitioners in the arts, sciences, and humanities.

Tanikawa's prodigious output is not confined to print. He participated in the conceptual design and creative process for the 1970 World's Fair in Osaka. He has been actively involved in creative endeavors in such media as photography, film, and video. He wrote several stage plays and nineteen movie scripts as well as a documentary film on the 1964 Tokyo Olympics. The 1972 documentary film on the Munich Olympics by the renowned Japanese film director, Ichikawa Kon, "Cease, Time, You Are Beautiful," was also created from a Tanikawa script. In 2008 he co-wrote and co-directed an unusual film for commercial distribution that combines poetry, still photos, and moving pictures to create a new type of movie.

In 2000 Tanikawa's enduring interest in modern technology led him to explore the then-new medium of multimedia for computers. He created and published a single CD-ROM disk that stores a collection of his works: the complete text of fifty-four volumes of poetry that he had published up to that point, selected English translations of his poems, video creations, audio readings, autobiographical notes, an extensive album of photos, a detailed bibliography, and excerpts of writing on his work by other poets and critics. The introduction in this present volume draws heavily on the contents of this disk.

Since then he has published several more volumes of poetry, notably *minimal* (2002), a collection of short-form poems; *Poet's Tomb* (2006), a ballad; and *Watashi* (*I Myself*) (2007). In 2009, he published *Tromsø Collage*, a collection of long narrative poems on varying themes.

Tanikawa's poetry has received a number of prestigious awards in Japan. He was awarded (but declined) the 6th Takami Jun Award for *Definitions* and *At Midnight in the Kitchen I Wanted to Talk to You*. Other honors include the 34th Yomiuri Literature Award for *The Map of Days*, the 26th Noma Children's Literature Award for *Naked*, the first Maruyama Yutaka Memorial Modern Poetry Award for *To a Woman*, the first Hagiwara Sakutarō Award for *Clueless*, and the first Ayukawa Nobuo Award for *Tromsφ Collage*. An active participant in international poetry festivals and events, Tanikawa leaves his footprints in all corners of the world. His poetry has been widely translated into English and many other European, Middle Eastern, and Asian languages, including Bulgarian, Hebrew, Macedonian, Mongolian, Nepalese, and Chinese.

Restarting Poetry in the Postwar World

To understand the impact and significance of Tanikawa's work, it is helpful to look at the state of poetry in general during the turmoil of post-WWII Japan from 1945 through 1952, when he published his first book of poetry.

On August 15, 1945, Japanese poets, like the general populace, found themselves facing a world turned upside down. World War II was over. Japan had surrendered to the allies, ceding control of the country to occupation forces under the Supreme Commander of Allied Powers (SCAP). In 1946 a new democratic Constitution of Japan, strongly influenced by SCAP, was promulgated. It took effect in May 1947, replacing the Meiji constitution of 1889 that had defined the Imperial reign. Japan's militaristic regime before and during WWII had used provisions of the Meiji constitution to suppress dissent and persecute the opposition. This included strict control and censorship of all kinds of speeches, activities, and publications. By contrast, the new constitution was idealistically democratic, establishing a range of human rights that included freedom of speech.

This does not mean that writers, publishers, broadcasters, and filmmakers were suddenly free to say whatever they wanted. SCAP imposed its own brand of censorship on the mass media and textbook publishers during the occupation. Its primary thrust was to ensure that these publications reflected democratic principles and that they did not publish material critical of the occupation. There was also a crackdown on pornography.

In the case of poetry, however, occupation censorship did not seem to be an issue. We find not a word about censorship in contemporary accounts of poetic activity, such as those by Kihara Kōichi, or in retrospectives written sixty years later. Instead poets felt liberated from their forced silence. Their sense of restored freedom sustained them through the hardships and devastation of the postwar years, charging them with energy to create new poetic movements and join forces to get their work published. Nagase Kiyoko, a poet who lived through most of the twentieth century, reminisced in her later years that "over 100 poetry magazines were published all over Japan during the years immediately following World War II."

Reading Kihara Kōichi's first-hand account of what he and his fellow poets accomplished in the wake of their liberation, we encounter an unquenchable thirst to find outlets for their creativity:

When the war ended, not a single poetry magazine was being published in Japan. In 1944, all the poetry magazines in Japan had been consolidated into two publications, *Japanese Poetry* and *The Study of Poetry*. The first issue of *The Study of Poetry* was June 27, 1944. I received it the day before I was to leave for Iwō Jima. I don't know how many issues were published after that. But it is the fact that for several months after the air raids on Tokyo started, neither *Japanese Poetry* nor *The Study of Poetry* were published. Their printing house and the publisher, Hōbunkan, had vanished in the air-raid fires.

Back then the only way left for poets to have their poetry read was to exchange poems by mail. In Tokyo, Kitazono Katsue and others formed *Mugi-Tsūshin* (*Wheat Correspondence*), and in Kyūshu Okada Yoshihiko and others had *Tsūshin* (*Correspondence*). There were some other groups as well, and poets were reading each other's work in secret. It was what you might call a supply line for minds in the middle of war. Many poets were drafted to be soldiers; some were stranded in foreign lands. Kuroda Saburō was in Java, Ayukawa Nobuo and Nakagiri Masao were hospitalized in Army hospitals, and Tamura Ryūichi was digging trenches in Ōtsu. As for me, I came back from Iwō Jima, just released from a hospital, and was feeling faint from malnutrition.

As if to break through this chaos, *FOU* was published in October 1945. It was *Correspondence* published in magazine form by Okada Yoshihiko and his cohorts. This was the first coterie poetry magazine published after WWII. Okada wrote in its inaugural issue: "In which direction is poetry starting out? We don't know until we write."

Kihara goes on to record year by year what he saw and experienced in the several years following. He recounts how, in the fall of 1946, he was invited to contribute his poetry to the magazine *Junsui-shi* (*Pure Poetry*). In reading its first issue he discovered that some poets younger than he had been writing throughout the war years, each in isolation.

Right after the December issue of *Pure Poetry* was published . . . the poets who contributed to this issue got together. Central to them were members of the former *LUNA* [coterie magazine] such as Ayukawa Nobuo, Nakagiri Masao, Tamura Ryūichi, Miyoshi Toyoichirō, and Kitamura Tarō. This was the day of my first reunion since the pre-war era with my fellow poets of *Arechi* (*Waste Land*). Ayukawa, in his leather jacket, spoke of his skepticism about modernism, casting his eyes on the floor. Tamura, in his navy-issue greatcoat, looked straight ahead and said, "What burned down were not only cities, but also our souls."

— *Eureka: Poetry and Criticism*, 1970, Tokyo

Arechi (*Waste Land*), the magazine of a major and powerful postwar poetry movement, was led by Ayukawa Nobuo, Tamura Ryūichi, and others.

The *Arechi* poets had become familiar with T. S. Eliot and "The Waste Land" before WWII, but faced with the post-WWII devastation, confusion, and despair prevalent in Japan, the term "waste land" took on a new significance. The poetry of the *Arechi* group was characterized by intense internal agony. Their mindscapes were full of the angst of their wartime experiences, colored deeply by desperation and desolation as evidenced by Tamura's words at their reunion. But their vision also implied the hope of rising above the rubble.

The members of the *Arechi* group were pioneers and a major force in post-WWII Japanese poetry. They were determined to depart from traditional poetics and past practices and succeeded in finding their own voices and establishing a new poetics. *Arechi Poems*, the first of their annual anthologies, was published in 1951, and continued through its eighth anthology in 1958.

A New Voice Appears

The poetic landscape in postwar Japan was marked by determination on the part of many participants to break away from the past in terms of both themes and forms. While the *Arechi* poets were making their mark in the 1950s, Japan was making progress toward economic recovery, and the people's outlook was turning more positive. It was against this backdrop that Tanikawa burst onto the scene.

His first book, *Alone in Two Billion Light Years,* was published in 1952, the year when the occupation ended and Japan started on the road to recovery and prosperity. The work represented a sharp break from the past, and the poets of the day took immediate notice. Ayukawa Nobuo, leader of the *Arechi* group, said of Tanikawa, "Away from existential or societal interest, he upholds transcendental aesthetics." Miyoshi Tatsuji, in the poem he wrote as a preface to the book, expresses the feeling that Tanikawa seems like someone who has suddenly arrived from another planet.

This young man
has come from a distant land, unexpected
he started out yesterday
from that somewhere far away
he journeyed a day
far longer than ten years,
without borrowing ten-thousand-mile shoes
how should we measure the distance he traveled
Just think
on a cold and frosty winter morning
all of a sudden, smiling,
something comes to us
would that be the stars sliding off this young man's notebooks?
Ah this daffodil . . .
its scent is cool and bittersweet
bearing the weight of being alone apt to tremble in the wind
with pride and modesty

. . .

Ah, this young man —
the one we have long hoped for
he is here suddenly from a distant land

This prefatory poem is especially notable for its emphasis on the "unexpectedness" and "suddenness" of Tanikawa's arrival. It also extols his poetry for its freshness and cosmic perspective.

Throughout the book Tanikawa's vision extended from the world around him to encompass the universe, as the title poem implies. *Alone in Two Billion Light Years* announced the arrival of a fresh, young, and excitingly promising poet, seemingly unaffected by the agonies and despair prevalent in poetry at the time. Sixteen years later, on the occasion of the publication of a volume of Tanikawa's collected poems to that point, the distinguished poet and critic Murano Shirō analyzed what Tanikawa's work represents in the context of post-WWII Japanese poetry.

Right from his first volume, *Alone in Two Billion Light Years*, no book of poetry in post WWII [Japan] has been as spectacular as

Tanikawa's. It is astounding to see that his poetry is so widely beloved, yet shows absolutely no sign of compromising in terms of poetry.

That is no doubt due to his uncommon insight and powerful creativity: specifically, his motifs are taken from the familiar details of modern life, which are quickly resolved into metaphysical experiences through the commanding viewpoint of a fresh and youthful perspective. In terms of superb intelligence and sharp wit no modern [Japanese] poet can surpass him. One can see his work as the archetype of a new modern [Japanese] poetry to succeed the poetry of the *Arechi* (*Waste Land*) group, whose movement is about to reach its completion.

— Tokyo Shinbun, 1968

Murano's comments show how distinctly Tanikawa's poetry stood out among that of his contemporaries in terms of intellect, insight, and popularity. Remarkably, several decades later, Tanikawa still stands alone at the pinnacle as an extraordinary presence among poets in Japan. He continues to receive the highest acclaim for his artistic achievements and enjoys an unprecedented measure of popularity among readers of all ages and walks of life.

His Poetry — The Art of Being Alone

Unlike poets just a few years older, Tanikawa is of a generation that was spared the psychological torment and despair of living under a repressive regime and experiencing the privations of war. Along with his upbringing, this circumstance fostered a more positive and expansive outlook than that of his predecessors. Since his first book of poetry appeared when Japan was in recovery mode, this outlook undoubtedly contributed to the quick and enthusiastic acceptance of his poems by the Japanese public.

However, we cannot ascribe the sustained popularity and quality of his poetry over the following decades to this initial impression of openness. He owes his continued success as a poet to his philosophical concept of life and art, and to the principled execution of his vision in his poetry.

Tanikawa has maintained a firm conviction that his poetry is independent of him as its author, however closely it may be modeled on the elements of his life. He talks about his "non-self" and references it to Keats, who espoused the "negative capability" of a poet, that is, the poet's ability to impartially create an independent voice that mirrors humanity, including the negative, undesirable aspects of existence. Also like Keats, Tanikawa creates and speaks through an alter ego, a poetic voice distinct from his own. His essays often assert the independence of a creation from its author, and he makes a point of distancing himself from his creation. Clearly he is taking a stand against conventional views, broadly held in Japan, of the relationship between a poet and his work. To understand the significance of his stance, it is helpful to look at a speech by Ōoka Makoto, poet and critic, whom Donald Keene calls "perhaps the finest [critic of poetry] in Japan today." Ōoka discusses the prevalent view of a poem's relationship with its author in terms of the nature of traditional Japanese poetry and its persistent influence on modern Japanese poetry:

> Though *haiku* might be far better known to foreign readers, it is very important to acknowledge that *waka* (*tanka*) has been the fundamental poetic form throughout the long tradition of Japanese poetry. Indeed, the form of *haiku* is derived from that of *waka*.
>
> The essence of *waka* comes out of those sensations we feel in everyday life. . . .
>
> While *haiku* can be called the crystallization of fugitive instants, one might call *waka* or *tanka* the endless lyrical stream of sentiments and thoughts experienced in everyday life.
>
> Contemporary poetry is a new kind of writing that differs from both *tanka* and *haiku*. Having come into existence nearly a century ago, and having no fixed form comparable to *tanka* or *haiku*, it has as its aim the free translation of meditations, complex feelings,

and a variety of observations which give personality to the modern age. The abundance of response here is difficult to contain in the condensed forms of *tanka* and *haiku*. . . .

Nevertheless we see in even the most modern poetry a traditionally deep tendency to express one's own feelings and thoughts as a modern man or woman from a modernized society in some very stylized way influenced by the long tradition of *tanka* and *haiku*.

> — *The Colors of Poetry: Essays on Classic Japanese Verse*, 1991

By standing firm with the concept of "non-self," and asserting independence from his creation, Tanikawa rejects the traditional stance that poetry must "express one's own feelings and thoughts."

Instead, he creates poetry through a skillful control of deceptively clear language. His words are so polished and so carefully selected that general readers may find his poetry attractive, casual, and easy to understand. But his fellow poets are often awed by his technical sophistication. The contemporary poet Yano Akiko describes it this way: "A very complex wiring is employed, but it's as if his methods and techniques are all hidden beneath the surface, which is itself fully covered by a pretty stainless material. That's the way I feel when I read [Tanikawa's poem], and I think to myself, 'Ah, wouldn't it be great if I could write a poem like that.'"

While the surface that encases Tanikawa's "complex wiring" is invariably smooth, his poetry is highly varied in terms of poetic modes. It encompasses lyrical poems, analytical prose poems, narrative poems, epic poems, satirical poems, and highly experimental poems. In virtually every book of poetry he consciously and artfully adopts a different style.

Fragments of a Forged Talamaikan Manuscript (translated in full in this book, see p. 111) may tell us why he does so. In this elaborately framed and sardonically annotated epic verse, Tanikawa fleshes out the concept that the genesis of poetry is rooted in primitive vocalization, the very origin of communication. These vocalizations could no doubt have taken many forms, and so does his poetry. For example, he concurrently wrote and published two books of poetry in diametrically opposed modes: *Definitions*, in which he uses studied expository prose for poetic expression, and *At Midnight in the Kitchen I Wanted to Talk to You*, in which he expresses his impromptu thoughts in seemingly casual speech.

He is just as liberal in his choice of poetic forms. In general Tanikawa uses Japanese traditional syllabic cadences sparingly and only for specific effects. He does use forms more familiar to English readers, such as sonnets, couplets, ballads and the like, though in his hands they differ markedly from their Western models. As with the sonnet, whose fourteen-line form was a receptacle for his profuse youthful energy, he uses these forms without their associated rhyme schemes or formal requirements, not only because the Japanese language does not adapt well to rhyming, but perhaps also because he would rather be free from all restrictions.

The Voice in His Poetry, from Birth to a Ripe Old Age

The voice of a poem, be it confessional, subjective, objective, or omniscient, is central to the poem's understanding and appreciation. While Tanikawa sees the voice in his poetry as independent of himself, the voice and its author have an intriguing relationship. Tracing how the voice fares and how it interacts with its author in different stages of his life will give us some perspective on the development of Tanikawa's poetry over the last half-century.

Birth of a Poet

The poem "Grass" is an epiphany. It is also an allegory of the birth of a poet.

and all at once
one time

> out of some place
> I was standing in this grass
> All I have to do
> was recorded in my cells
> That is why I took the shape of a man
> and even talked about happiness
> — Grass (*translated by W. S. Merwin with Takako Lento*)

In this quiet but dramatic manner a poet comes into existence on earth, out of some unknown place, all alone, fated to carry the weight of his humanity and to express aspects of human life. To this poet, writing poetry is part of his nature, in sync with Nature's rhythm:

> Isn't it the case that desiring to make a poem is the same as letting a tree grow? It is as natural as our receiving life, being born.
> — "To the Cosmos! — an agitation" 1959

Tanikawa took this open and expansive stance in part because of the circumstances of his formative years. In a dialogue with Ayukawa Nobuo, leader of the *Arechi* group, whose poetry and poetics were so heavily influenced by their war-time experience, Tanikawa emphasizes the difference between his background and theirs:

> I did not go to the War. I have no experience with the military. I was spared the group relocations that were forced on kids a few years older than I was. Kids of my age were commuting from home to attend school, and in place of school work we helped older kids in their preparation to be relocated. On top of that I was an only child, born in a relatively well-to-do family, and grew up quite sheltered. During the War, too, I was not directly affected by it, protected by the shields my parents placed around me. So on top of growing up as an only child, I had no experience of being thrown into a group of people as I would have had in group relocation, or of having to survive through interpersonal struggles. Somehow I was so alone. . . .

Notable in this remark is that not only does he say he had no immediate experience with the war and wartime events, but also that he had no experience in interpersonal struggles. These were the formative experiences as well as a source of creative energy for writers who were his immediate predecessors.

He also talks about his sense of freedom from literary history or tradition in a dialogue with Ōoka Makoto, who was born in the same year as Tanikawa:

> I thought I had nothing to do with history. I firmly, maybe strangely, believed that history is something one can simply discard, and that if one is to write poetry, a genuine poetry would have to come out of a barren land. That barren land certainly would have nourishing soil to allow seeds to germinate, but the land to me was silent, and not something one could take in through analysis.
>
> So when I started writing poetry, I never paid any attention to where I was in relation to the history of Modern Japanese poetry, or in relation to the history of the world.
>
> — *Physiology of Criticism,* 1984

Here we have a creative mind, starting his career as a writer, standing free of the complex literary and psychological struggles that most other Japanese writers grappled with during the first decade after WWII. In this sense Tanikawa stood alone among the poets and writers of his time.

Thus devoid of the source of energy other writers derived from their wartime struggles, Tanikawa's mind focused on the philosophical contemplation of his being, Nature, the world, the universe, or the Cosmos. He sees his existence as part of Nature, which in turn is part of the Cosmos. He explains this concept and the significance of the Cosmos in a dialogue with his father, the philosopher Tanikawa Tetsuzō.

> **Tetsuzō**: What is your concept of the Cosmos? It seems clear, but at the same time not so clear.

> **Shuntarō**: When I use the word "Cosmos," it is pointing to a vast universe of which human life is only one part, probably influenced somewhat by [D.H.] Lawrence. This concept of the Cosmos, I believe, was nurtured by my living in the midst of Nature in Kita-Karuizawa in my youth. In my late teens and early twenties, I experienced a state where I was completely absorbed in Nature, where being one with Nature was to be alive, and where I felt so genuinely happy and whole. In that context I wanted to refer to that state, not by the term Nature, but as the Cosmos, meaning to capture the entirety of myself and Nature. Human life that has evolved from inorganic matter, a planet called Earth, and other stars scattered in the sky are all connected in my mind. It is a sort of pantheism that I believe in.
>
> — "Dialogues with Tanikawa Tetsuzō," 1974

In these conversations we see a significant correspondence between the birth of the poet in the allegory of "Grass" and the making of Tanikawa Shuntarō as a poet in real life. Given this correspondence, and given also the strong influence traditional Japanese poetry has on modern Japanese poetry, as outlined by Ōoka in the speech quoted earlier, it is tempting to assume that poet and the voice in his poetry are one and the same, in other words, to assume the "I" in the poem is Tanikawa Shuntarō. This reading of Tanikawa's poetry is reinforced by the lucidity of his poetic style and his personal presence, seemingly easily accessible and unassuming. And that is exactly how many of his readers, including critics, do read his poetry. Of course it is perfectly fine to enjoy the dazzling clarity of the presentation at this most overt level. But to truly appreciate Tanikawa's poetry and his achievements, we must move beyond reading his poems as spontaneous outpourings of his own thoughts and feelings.

Poet as Persona

Tanikawa is a superbly skilled and conscious artist, and his presence within his poetry is surprisingly elusive. Tanikawa Shuntarō, the author, deliberately distances himself from the "I" in his poetry. This is by design, as he explains in his short piece titled "I":

> . . . The relationship between a poem and its author, the poet, is far more complex and subtle as well as more fluid than normally assumed. A piece of poetry certainly will not be produced without its author's real-life experience. But are the thoughts and feelings expressed in the poetry actually held by its author in real life? In many cases that is not necessarily so. Poetry is not a tool to convey thoughts, or a place to express opinions. Nor is it even a means of self-expression. . . . If viewed only from the angle of the author's intent and message, "I" in a poem cannot be understood.

Here Tanikawa is making a clear and definitive statement that the voice in his poetry should be understood as separate and independent from himself, even though he uses his own life experience to create the voice. This voice celebrates youth, matures, and ages more or less in sync with the stages of Tanikawa's own life. But the "I" in his poetry, whom I will refer to as "the Poet" in this essay, is a persona distinct from Tanikawa.

Tanikawa subtly teases the reader on this distinction. Take, for example, the last sonnet in his second book of poems, *62 Sonnets*.

62

Because the Cosmos embraces me with love
(heartlessly, or at times
tenderly)
I can be alone for ever

When a woman was granted me for the first time
I was just listening for the resonance of the Cosmos
Only simple sorrows and joys are clear to me
because I always belong to the Cosmos

I throw myself
at the sky, at the tree, at the woman

all soon to be part of the abundance of the Cosmos itself
. . . I call to her
then the Cosmos looks back
and I am no more

In an unusually direct and open account of what he intended to express in the poem, Tanikawa explicates it in a way that makes it clear that his reality is different from what the poem presents.

62 Sonnets is a book that celebrates my youth. I am confident that I was the epitome of youth, and that I was able to be faithful to my youthfulness. These sonnets flowed naturally out of me, as if they were made of my youthfulness itself. . . .

First, the word *sekai* in the first line is not "the world" but "the Cosmos." I believed in [D.H.] Lawrence and was dreaming of the sun and the moon within myself. While I understood how indifferent the universe is to us, I trusted in the benevolence of the riches of our planet. I had a physical sensation of being one with the Cosmos. That is expressed in the following two lines

(heartlessly, or at times
tenderly).

"Alone" in the fourth line refers to human aloneness. I had not yet known a human-to-human bond, therefore I was ignorant about genuine human solitude. This line reflects the arrogance rooted in my youthful conviction that the Cosmos is embracing me with love, but at the same time it reflects the peace in my mind generated from being in Nature in the summer hills. "When a woman was granted me for the first time" refers, in specific terms, to my first experience in love.

". . . resonance of the Cosmos" is an abstraction from the sound of ripples beating at the edge of a pond, the sound of the wind blowing across woods, the calls of birds at night. This line reveals that I did not yet attach human meaning to my love experience.

Let me add that, in *62 Sonnets*, I differentiate between the word *hito* [in cursive syllabary] meaning a woman, and the word *hitobito* [in ideograms] indicating people. The next two lines

> Only simple sorrows and joys are clear to me
> because I always belong to the Cosmos

say that I still belong to the Cosmos due to my youth, and am indifferent to human psychological complexity. *This of course does not relate directly to me in real life at that time. I was more human in my real life.* [emphasis added]

In the next line, by juxtaposing three things, "at the sky, at the tree, at her," I wanted to indicate that the woman was also part of the Cosmos. The line "I throw myself" refers to physically throwing myself at all of them, but at the same time it relates to the line "soon to be part of the abundance of the Cosmos itself" referring to the meaning of youthful actions. This is hedonistic in a way, but I had a desire to deliberately throw myself into the Cosmos, to release my narcissistic self into the larger entirety, which I believe is also expressed in the last stanza of this poem. In the lines

> . . . I call to her
> then the Cosmos looks back
> and I am no more

I was trying to capture a human being in existential, rather than social, terms.

— "To the Cosmos!"

In the middle of presenting this cosmic communion, overflowing with youthful energy, Tanikawa casually and cheerfully asserts, *"This of course does not relate directly to me in real life at that time. I was more human in my real life."* We sense the dry humor with which Tanikawa is playing with us, his unsuspecting readers. He discusses what he intended the "I" in the poem to speak of, as if the voice in the poem is his own. Then he suddenly distances himself from the "I" in the poem, and we are forced to face that disconnect, and left feeling as if we were watching a life-size puppet handled by a crafty puppeteer dressed just like the puppet he is handling. This generates a subtle yet intriguing dramatic irony. As Tanikawa puts it, "the relationship between a poem and its author, the poet, is far more complex and subtle as well as more fluid than normally assumed." Indeed, the relationship between Tanikawa and his persona is highly complex, as his persona, the Poet, reflects, refracts, and projects the deeper psyche of his puppeteer, namely Tanikawa Shuntarō.

Tanikawa's whole career can be seen as a journey taken in the company of his poetic voice, whom we call the Poet. He states the purpose of this journey as early as 1959:

> In terms of poetry, I have long had a seemingly odd conviction that what really matters to me is not necessarily poetry per se, but the relationship between life and words.
>
> — "To the Cosmos!"

In this context "life" refers to man's day-to-day life, his thoughts, his imagination, the world around him, Nature, and the universe; and "words" are not things neatly defined in dictionaries, but organic entities that are intrinsically connected with "life" in the depths of human psyche. "Coca Cola Lesson" (p. 137) indelibly dramatizes this connection. A boy, sitting on a jetty feeling splashing sea waves on his ankles, "visualized in his mind the word 'Sea' and the word 'Me' at the very same time." As he mindlessly tosses those two words around, something odd happens:

> The word "Sea" grew bigger and bigger in his head, and brimmed over to merge into the sea in front of him the way two drops of water would, and suddenly they dissolved into one.
>
> At the same time, the word "Me" grew smaller and smaller like the tip of a thin needle, but never disappeared. Rather, the smaller it grew, the brighter it gleamed, moving from his head down toward his center, now floating like a single speck of plankton in the "Sea" that converged with the sea.

Here we see the boy experience the word "Sea" as concept converging with the real sea with irresistible energy while "Me," the core of his being, stays firmly at the center. The boy's experience points to what Tanikawa means when he writes "what really matters to me . . . is the relationship between life and words." And to Tanikawa this is the making of genuine poetry.

Time and again Tanikawa uses the sea as a metaphor for words. The Poet often gazes out to the sea, hears its roar, or tries to peer into its dark depths, as he is destined to pursue a perfect union between what he sees and what comes to him and emerges from him as words.

Three Stages in the Life of the Poet

The Poet's focus and concerns naturally change over time. As a young man, the Poet is enamored with the Cosmos, which in turn "embraces him with love." Conceiving of his existence as part of the vast Cosmos, disassociated from other human beings on earth, he inevitably faces an intense awareness of being alone. This serves to drive his youthful creativity, which he expresses with words that seem to flow endlessly out of him. In his prime the Poet celebrates his physical being and his family, and he is mindful of his worldly acclaim. But his mind is not satisfied. As he tries to write poetry, words fail him, and the poetry he is after remains out of reach. His pursuit is relentless, and the ensuing struggles with words keep intensifying. His struggles eventually become his central focus and cause the Poet to feel an agonizing sense of inability. As the Poet ages, his focus is more on his aging self, and he carefully studies the condition of being in the dusk of one's life. Yet he is still in pursuit of genuine poetry.

In the following three sections of this essay we will attempt to trace how the Poet fares at each stage of his life. "The Poet as a young man" focuses mainly on *Alone in Two Billion Light Years* (1952) and *62 Sonnets* (1953), "Midlife crisis" on *Journey* (1968/1995), and "The dusk of life" on *minimal* (2002).

The Poet as a Young Man: Alone and One with the Cosmos

Alone in Two Billion Light Years was published in 1952 when Tanikawa was twenty-one years old. This first book of poetry appeared like a sudden revelation in the post-WWII poetry scene in Japan and was spectacularly successful in both popular and critical terms.

Its phenomenal reception was due to at least two elements: Tanikawa's style and his underlying philosophical conviction. The style is elegant, smooth, so clear that any reader, young or old, would feel it was easy to read and understand. Yet its simple surface masks considerable depths. The more you read, the deeper its implications. This explains the enthusiasm his readers of all ages seem to maintain throughout their lives.

Through this seemingly effortless style Tanikawa communicates his concept of existence relative to the Cosmos, not as a brainy philosophical thesis, but as the almost visceral and empirical conviction of being one with the universe, which is expressed in his conversation with his philosopher father. The basis of this concept, even though presented in Tanikawa's distinctive manner, is universally understood throughout the world in both religious and philosophical contexts. It speaks to the very core of human hearts and minds.

The title poem "Alone in Two Billion Light Years" (p. 45) typifies how these elements work. The Poet's voice is calm and matter of fact, using simple words. He speaks of people on the planet earth and inhabitants of the imagined world on Mars gravitating to one another. He draws us into a feeling of cosmic attraction as well as unease. Then, he sneezes. Suddenly we feel the Poet standing right next to us, and we face the span of two billion light years, both of us feeling deeply alone. The experience is emotionally gripping, yet transcendent.

In the teacher's manual for a Junior High "Modern Japanese" textbook, Tanikawa explained what "two billion light years" means:

"Two billion light years" means the diameter of the universe based on my knowledge at that time. It was not that I was particularly interested in astronomy. As a 19-year-old, having grown up as the only child in a fortunate environment, I did not yet know solitude in the social context, and I seemed to think of myself as a single piece of organic substance thrown out into the limitless Universe, and to define my state as "being alone" without attaching to it any emotional dimensions such as feelings of loneliness or pity in isolation.

Note that Tanikawa uses the word *kodoku* [孤独] for what is translated as "being alone." The word consists of two ideograms: *"ko"* meaning "alone," and *"doku,"* meaning "by oneself," roughly translated. So although *kodoku* is often associated in general usage with feelings of loneliness or sadness at being isolated, it means literally "being alone and by oneself." Hence Tanikawa's notation that the Poet's use of the word is totally neutral with no emotional baggage such as loneliness or pity. However, general readers will interpret this poem in various ways that relate to their own experience, and appreciate the poem accordingly. Many would initially associate the poem with a sense of forlornness at being alone, but at some point the same readers might come to share the Poet's more cosmic view. Even to a young reader the poem would point to an experience beyond simple loneliness, if only subconsciously.

Tanikawa explains the source and nature of "being alone" in relation to his own experience, explicating the Poet's reality in the poem. The conviction of being one with the Cosmos, shared by him and the Poet, is central to his earlier poems such as "To Go Home" (p. 127):

I was made from a bit of Heaven and Earth
There was no need to blow the breath of life into me
because both Heaven and Earth were breathing

In this poem the Poet is given life as part of Heaven and Earth, as an immediate kin to a chestnut tree in his backyard, and finds happiness not among people but as part of the orderly cosmos, which he knows will take him back as its own when he is no more. He is naturally and unquestionably part of the Cosmos. It is his birthright. His existence is like a dew drop in the morning: a sphere so vulnerable and transient yet capable of holding in itself the entirety of the sky and the earth while it is in the world.

This poem is among a group subtitled "Poems written when the poet was 21 or 22 years old" in his *Second Collected Poems,* published in 1979. In it he puts the notation "the Cosmos" in phonetic transliteration next to the word *"sekai,"* which is normally translated as "the world." Why did he choose to do this, instead of simply using the corresponding Japanese word for the Cosmos? Perhaps Tanikawa chose to give the single word a double layer of significance: the Poet's immediate physical world and the Cosmic world.

As part of the cosmos, though it "embraces [him] with love," the young Poet is keenly aware of the transience of life in time and space within the cosmic order. In his sonnet 19, "Vastness" (p. 51), as he feels the wind rising and senses time stirring, he knows that "its subtle motion too / will soon be forgotten." He is determined to maintain that mental perspective.

In "Spring" (p. 45), even when he is looking at a perfectly peaceful and pleasant Spring scene from a train window, he does not miss "the chimney of a nursing home." But he consciously trades "[his] momentary fatalism / for the scent of plum blossoms."

Through these poems we hear the voice of a youth, thoughtful yet full of wonder at what he sees in life. Later Tanikawa recalls how profusely productive he was when he was young.

Of course content may determine its form. But in my case, a poetic form is also important. Take, for example, my second book of poetry *62 Sonnets* (1953). Back then when I went to Kita-Karuizawa [where his family villa was located], words upon words would just flow out of me. I would cram them into a sonnet form of fourteen lines, and I came up with about one hundred sonnets.

— *I Have Been Writing Poetry This Way,* 2010

The youthful poet had faith in himself and his expansive view of the Cosmos, and words came to him in a rush to express his thoughts and emotions in poetry.

Midlife Crisis: Poetry, Silence, and Words

As he comes to the prime of his life, the Poet faces an internal conflict between how he is seen as a poet and the true poet he desires to be. Nature to him is no longer part of the all-inclusive Cosmos that once embraced him with love and allowed him to sing freely. Now its presence and beauty render him speechless, figuratively and literally.

In the book titled *Journey* we see the earnest and agonizing pilgrimage of a poet as he tries to be true to poetry, to his creativity, and to his medium, words. The Poet speaks of his internal conflict against the backdrop of the places he visits. The first group of poems in *Journey* is titled "Toba 1~10 and addendum." Toba is a region on an inlet from the Pacific Ocean. The home of pearl fishers, it boasts intricate shorelines and emerald water. The name Toba itself conjures up an idyllic and profoundly satisfying existence. The image of a poet in this setting, pained by his inability to re-create ultimate beauty with words, is fitting, captivating, and even romantic. The second group, titled "Trip 1~8," is from his travels overseas; some of the pieces have place names associated with them. Here again the Poet speaks of what he saw and felt in each place, and of his inner struggles with words. The last group, titled "anonym 1~8," presents the Poet's ultimate resolve to grapple with true poetry as he sees it. The title probably symbolizes his desire to become the unidentifiable medium that itself conveys silence, the ultimate poetry.

Overall, *Journey* presents us with a portrait of a poet grappling with the most important and difficult issues any poet can face, and resolving to stick to his mission: to be true to his creative ideal. The process begins with "Toba."

In the face of a Nature which renders him speechless with its "everlasting radiance," the Poet knows that the "radiance" is what he has to capture and communicate with words ("Toba 1," p. 73).

> Other than this quiet at the height of the day
> I have nothing I want to tell you about
> even if you are bleeding in your country
> Ah, this everlasting radiance!

The Poet sounds pained and frustrated. Though in the prime of life, he feels inner conflicts and self-doubt to the extent that he even confesses that he is not actually a poet, at least not in the way he wishes to be. All he wants to talk about is "this quiet at the height of the day" with the sun, the boulders and the sea in "this everlasting radiance!" That "quiet" is poetry. The Poet is totally immersed in this quiet, and he finds himself speechless. How can one capture this silence with words? To find the answer is his mission, and the source of his agony. In the midst of glorious Nature and his wholesome family, the Poet is in silent agony and despair. The Poet tells us about his agony in more direct terms in "Toba 5" (p. 75).

> Words do not ride in the wind
> Words do not appear on paper
> They do not come to me
>
> . . .
> If there is any bitterness leveled against me
> that is silence, nothing else

The words that flowed out of the Poet in abundance in his youthful years seem to have lost their energy. They simply do not come to him. He now has to deal with a dark unyielding sea of words. He sees a boat coming back from the sea. To the Poet, the boat represents a glimpse of hope moving toward him but he cannot see the oarsman who should have been steering the boat, and who might have shown him his true direction. So the Poet is resolved to be self-reliant, or to "answer to [his] own being." This is a turnabout from the Poet's youthful days when his sight was fixed on the limitless space that contained his being. He is now trying to look into his self, and intends to verbally examine self for the words he needs.

But the Poet finds this exploration desperately difficult. He later confides his pain to a friend, and his wish for release from it. In a poem dedicated to Kanaseki Hisao, a writer and scholar of American literature, the Poet starts with a quote from John Berryman ("14," p. 104).

"I am obliged to perform. . . .
operations of great delicacy
on my self."
Was that Berryman, who killed himself?

The quote is from poem #67 of John Berryman's *The Dream Songs*, in which its narrator and protagonist Henry speaks of his need to conduct "in complete darkness / operations of great delicacy / on my self," to dissect his own persona. In Berryman's poem Henry seems satisfied with the outcome, at least for the moment: "My / friend, I succeeded. Later." Tanikawa's Poet, by contrast, remains in agony. When he tries to bring the words he finds within him out into the open air, they betray him, turning into "a vampire under the sun." In despair he wishes to be lost in a stupor, where there is no need for words.

At this stage he can no longer trust words, but he will not give up pursuing them even if that effort seems overwhelming, as the Poet says in "Toba 6" (p. 76). The Sea is again a metaphor for words in the sense we saw in "Coca Cola Lesson" (p. 128).

Sea —
even this single word contains deceit
But I insist on saying it
facing the waves rising before a storm

In the course of his relentless pursuit of the right words, the Poet tries to find comfort in his wife's embrace, but all he gets is a primal groan that seems like a "sweet murmur" to his ears while the sea is still at a distance:

But we groan

> The groan is now a sweet murmur
> to my heated ear, closer than the sea

The Poet's struggle is brought to the forefront at the end of Toba series (see "Toba addendum," p. 79).

> Just now Inspiration ran past me
> leaving me with a meager amount of words
> not to convey something
> the words are writhing like infants

Even Inspiration leaves him with only a few feeble words, which are simply "writhing like infants." With words no longer abundantly flowing out of him, he needs to reach for them. But now it requires formidable effort: "A journey to words / is as far and uncertain as a journey to Mars." As we saw in "Alone in Two Billion Light Years" (p. 47), when he was young he felt close to Mars as a co-inhabitant of the Cosmos, but it now seems so distant and forbidding. He even tries to grab onto words from what he has considered the ossified past, but that fails too:

> And thrown at me for the first time
> are the words from you of bleached bones
> They are
>
> . . .
>
> I cannot come up with them

His pain and his sense of powerlessness are palpable in these lines.

What does "poetry" mean to the Poet, then? In a series of poems titled Trip 1~8, he tries to tell us (pp. 79–84). On the surface, for example, "Trip 7" is a celebration of the beauty and harmony of the scenery the Poet encounters on his trip, and of the Poet's resolve to reach the silence of timelessness through his writing. He invites readers to imagine and share the breathtaking beauty and calm beyond his words. For the Poet, however, this is not a simple matter. He is tormented by his own inability to capture beauty and truth with words, yet he is still determined to "arrive at this silence / by polishing words." The Poet seeks to capture the eternal moment, true poetry, seemingly with some hope.

Later he observes a farmer who seamlessly blends in with the quiet that prevails over the complete beauty of Nature. Standing in the shadow of a tall young tree, the Poet is so self-conscious about his inability to write that he thinks that even the farmer, as if he were omniscient, "knows how [the Poet] failed to write when [he] tried." He feels dejected again (see "Trip 8," p. 84).

Yet the Poet does not give up. In "anonym 1" (p. 84) he speaks of his resolve to be a poet.

> If I stay silent
> I must say I am silent
> If I cannot write
> I must write that I cannot write

Haunted by his failure to capture silence through words, in "anonym 3"(p. 86) he senses a possible approach to silence in "breath," which he believes is the source of poetry as well as music —

> From the closed cave
> in the depth of your chest
> breath comes out
> to mix with the Spring air

and surrenders to Music in "anonym 4" (p. 86).

> Silence contains
> just words
>
> The edges of clouds shine in gold
> Music
> seduces me

What he wants to capture in words is extremely elusive. He tries to describe it in "anonym 6" (p. 87).

> it's like a scent
> it's just here, but no longer here
> it's not here, but brimming over
> like Time

And as words fail to come to him he even caricatures himself as a creature of myth, eternally silent:

> With my elbows on my desk
> with my eyes staring at the wall
> I am a Sphinx . . .

In the last of the "anonym" series, however, the Poet turns his ears to the primal source of communication among people ("anonym 8," p. 88):

> Breaths become turbulent thoughts
> Thoughts turn into heavy sighs
> . . .
> That somehow brings about songs
> The songs once again return
> to the tangled breaths of the multitude

Breaths are the source of life and energy, allowing us to think, leading us to mumble, then to scream in frustration, where "ultimately words are undefined." The silence in breaths is energy, bottled up and concentrated, as in "cries of falling leaves, the wailing of the blue sky, howls from piles and piles of corpses," and these are begging to be released and defined with words. The Poet is no longer in despair, even though he is not free of his struggle. Hearing cries, wailing, and screams, he is determined to take them on.

Journey was first published in 1968 as twenty-five poems of fourteen lines, each accompanied by original art. It was received with great enthusiasm by general readers, and caused a commotion among poets. Some poets took issue with the lines "Let me tell you the truth / I am not a poet

/ though I pretend to be one," and wondered out loud why Tanikawa, prolific and by far the most popular and successful poet in Japan, would make such a statement. Some questioned his motives, and others even seemed to feel that Tanikawa was disingenuous in writing these words in his poem. All this was said in spite of Tanikawa's protestations that the Poet in his poetry is not his own self. In other words, many of his fellow poets were unwilling to accept the premise that those words are uttered by the Poet, that is, Tanikawa's persona, not by the real-life Tanikawa.

Tanikawa makes a point of this in his dialogue with Yoshimasu Gōzō, a well-known Japanese poet of the succeeding generation, as recorded in the supplement to the expanded 1995 edition of *Journey*:

> *Y:* What surprised me was the line, "my wife is beautiful". . .
> *T:* Everyone teased me about that so much. Their teasing
> reminded me that I wrote that as a complete fiction. But
> people refused to read it as fiction. I was amused by that.

The fact that no one read his lines as fictitious illustrates Tanikawa's unique standing in the literary scene of his time, or for that matter in modern Japanese poetry. *Journey* created a stir in part because his fellow poets had a hard time accepting the voice in poetry to be independent of its creator. It marked a clear departure from what was—and still is—generally assumed to be poetry: an outpouring of its author's own emotions and thoughts.

Tanikawa regards the 1995 publication as the final complete edition of *Journey*. There are significant differences from the original 1968 edition. He added "anonym 7" and "anonym 8," for a total of twenty-seven poems. Also it was published as a two-volume set rather than a single book. The main volume, called *Journey,* contains just the poems with his postscript. The second volume, "supplement," is a monograph containing English translations (by William Elliot and Kazuo Kawamura) of the twenty-seven poems, the dialogue on *Journey* between Tanikawa and Yoshimasu, and essays or comments on the first edition of *Journey* by contemporary poets. The essays and comments give us a taste of the commotion the original publication had generated.

In his postscript to this final edition, Tanikawa explains why it was is-sued nearly three decades after the original.

> It has been 26 years since the publication of *Journey* with illustra-tive art work. Why do I re-publish such an old book of poetry? It is not simply because the book is out of print. The series of 14-liners titled "Journey" consists of 27 poems, but they had not yet been published as an independent book of poetry as a whole. The ear-lier *Journey* with artwork does not contain "anonym 7" and "ano-nym 8," which I wrote later. Other volumes of selected poems con-tain only portions of *Journey*.
>
> Also many people have commented on *Journey* since it was first published. From the point of view of its author, looking back, it seems to mark a turning point in my career. If I am allowed to be a bit self-indulgent, I might say that *Journey* seems to have some significance in the history of modern Japanese poetry. With these thoughts in mind, I would like to present this book to readers. . . .

Though Tanikawa's words are typically modest, he is clearly aware of where this book stands relative to the course of modern Japanese po-etry. He "re-published" *Journey* as a complete edition, to re-state his declaration of independence, so to speak, from the conventional views and practices of the poetry of his time.

Dusk of Life: Poem in Tatters

In *minimal*, published in 2002, the Poet's focus is fixed on the dusk of life. The tone throughout is quiet and thoughtful, and resigned. Yet he is still yearning for genuine poetry. "Tatters" (p. 168), the first poem in the book, sets the tone. In the twilight a personified Poem "robed in tat-tered words" comes to the Poet. Because of the reference to "offering" in the following lines, the Poem in tatters takes on the likeness of a hum-ble Buddhist monk begging for sustenance. The Poet feels that he has nothing to offer, but can only gratefully receive Poem's benevolence. As he is allowed a glimpse of Poem's naked self, a glimpse of a genuine poem, the Poet does not pursue it. The Poet no longer shows his agonizing creative urge. He simply "mends" the tattered words.

In "Just the way it is" (p. 173), the Poet is now aged, and feels the presence of a dead friend, as if he is seeing the friend preparing for a trip. But he has been left behind, in the town, as isolated as ever:

> Everything moves on
> just the way it is
> heading toward memories

The portrait in "I sit" (p. 171) is stark senility personified. Yet somehow there is a warm acceptance of that state.

> One afternoon with the sky covered in thin clouds
> I sit on a sofa
> like a shelled clam

The sky is no longer limitlessly blue and absorbing, as it was in "Billy the Kid." Thin clouds intervene. In light diffused through the clouds, the Poet is small, exposed, and helpless. He no longer has the energy to act, but is simply "sitting enchanted." The only saving grace is that everything seems beautiful and wondrous to him.

This is in striking contrast to "14" from *At Midnight I Wanted to Talk to You*, in which the Poet confided his wish to escape into a stupor from his struggles with words. In his prime, the imagined stupor had its own attraction, offering hope for release from his agony, but now he really is in a state of stupor and he passively marvels at all things around him.

Or is his self-image his own shadow? (See "My shadow," p. 171.)

> Turning into my own shadow
> I walk along a reddish brown wall
>
> . . .
>
> Wishing to dissolve
> things with physical form
> into thin air

In his youth, he believed trees were his brothers. Now as a river flows away, the trees send it off, bowing their heads. The Poet seems to see the river as his life taking its course, sent off by those trees that once shared the joy of his birth. He is now a shadow of his own being, and he is waiting to slip into thin air, the quiet (or nothingness) of sleep.

In "And then" (p. 172) death is a relief, "a divine grace," in the eternally recurring seasons. Yet while distant things are getting hazy, the Cosmos is still "at his nose." The Poet's youthful imagination still haunts him in the dusk of his life.

He even speaks for an insignificant pebble on a child's palm (see "A pebble," p. 178).

resting
in a trance
on a child's palm

I roll off
to where there is no shame

Rounded by the passage of time, the pebble now reflects the sky, resting enchanted on an innocent palm, and is about to roll off to a place where there is no self-consciousness. Is this pebble the Poet himself? If so, is this an ideal state of being, or the inevitable ending of an insignificant existence?

The Poet sees his face, the unique face of his fate, in the mirror (see "Face," p. 179). Looking deeper still, he tries to identify "a faint light" he sees in its depths. He is apparently hoping to find "another face" there, but is left frustrated, unable to succeed in his effort. The other face is probably the face of the true poet he desires to be, but to his eyes it is as fleeting as genuine poetry.

The idea of "the last sunrise" is captivating. The sun will rise to break the day and to bring daylight into "the night of [his] heart." We recall how a poem came to him "before daybreak," yet the Poet is calling it the "last sunrise" here. Is it hope or despair? This is a persistent ambiguity. In "As I am doing now," the Poet is "at a small boat landing," probably having come down the river to the river mouth. Something as heavy as wet sand is weighing on his mind. As he follows a trail he finds it leading to "a headland," stretching out to the sea. He is once again facing the sea. Is it with hope or with despair this time?

Poet as Chameleon

Tanikawa's "postscript" to *minimal* gives us a clue as to how his lifelong belief in the distance between poet and poem ultimately led him to a new mode of expression:

> . . . I came to feel it somewhat distasteful to see myself writing poetry with such ease, and looking at reality only through the eyes of poetry. . . .
>
> . . . When the late Tsuji Yukio invited me to his gatherings, *Yo-haku-kukai* [Marginal *Haiku* Gatherings], I occasionally dropped in for fun. My hope, probably, was to find some pathway that might lead me to genuine reality. Not through modern poetry, but by way of *haiku,* a short traditional form which I had long resisted. But as I was writing *haiku,* I came to realize that the form was absolutely too short for me.
>
> In the meantime I had an opportunity to travel to China. In the leisurely moments of a relaxed journey, some unexpected short poems popped up in me. Before I realized it, I might have become attuned to the direct opposite of wordiness, that is, in tune with *haiku* and possibly in tune with a certain type of classic Chinese poetry. . . .
>
> I believe what led me to the short form, which had been foreign to me, was my subconscious desire to be silent, and my desire to return to silence to start writing anew. But I am not sure if I myself have changed, along with the poetic form. Keats said that a poet is a chameleon and that the poet's essence is non-self. I will not forget his words until the day I die.

Here he speaks about "finding a pathway to genuine reality," because he feels shielded from genuine reality by writing poetry with such "ease." But isn't "genuine reality" simply the "creative ideal / genuine poetry," or "the silence" that the Poet has been seeking throughout his struggles?

In any event, at this time he arrived at a shorter form of poetry by way of his new interest in *haiku*, and a similar interest in a certain type of Chinese poetry. These poetic forms both make extremely economical and evocative use of words, leaving much unsaid. This offers him the hope of satisfying his "subconscious desire to be silent, and desire to return to silence to start writing anew."

At this point one life-cycle of the Poet as a persona seems complete. Tanikawa is now looking to a continuum on the horizon, facing the same sea, but with a fresh outlook, changing colors like a chameleon. He is as elusive as ever, professing his belief in "non-self," referring to John Keats who wrote:

A Poet is the most unpoetical of any thing in existence; because he has no Identity—he is continually in for—and filling some other Body—The Sun, the Moon, the Sea and Men and Women who are creatures of impulse are poetical and have about them an un-changeable attribute—the poet has none; no identity—he is cer-tainly the most unpoetical of all God's Creatures. . . . not one word I ever utter can be taken for granted as an opinion growing out of my identical nature—how can it, when I have no nature?
—Letter to Richard Woodhouse, October 27, 1818

In 2006 Tanikawa published a book-length ballad, *Poet's Tomb*. In a gentle, flowing rhythm it weaves a story of a young poet and the young woman who falls in love with his poetry. The young poet writes beauti-ful incidental poetry to order for all occasions for everyone, and receives high acclaim. But when the young woman pursues him as a person, he turns invisible. She sees the living world right through him, and she finds herself standing by his old tomb with no epitaph.

Is this ballad a caricature of a popular poet, or is it telling us an allegory of how the poet is fated to be a mere invisible medium for the living world? One can argue for either reading, or for something else entirely.

Watashi (*I Myself*) was published in 2007. In Japanese *"watashi"* is the core word for first person singular pronouns, corresponding to the English pronouns "I," "my," "me," and "mine." Traditional Japanese culture called for such self-effacement that one would customarily omit the subject "I" in conversation or even in writing. This time-honored practice persists in contemporary Japan. From this standpoint, for a Japanese poet to make one's self the central presence is quite daring.

This, however, does not mean that we get to meet Tanikawa straight on. Though he announces himself to be at center stage in this book and may seem to have shed his puppeteer's role, Tanikawa the author remains elusive. Each poem here simply points to an aspect of *watashi* as seen from a different angle, and together they form a kaleidoscopic mapping of a poet's mindscape.

The title piece is a series of eight poems. It starts with his self-introduction, in which he seems to present himself objectively: his appearance, preferences, and activities. But he writes, "All the above are facts, but once I put them down in words like this, somehow they do not ring true." This reminds us of his despair in midlife over "the words in his soul" turning into "a vampire under the sun." At the very outset we get fair warning that we are being invited into the gray zone between real and unreal.

The third poem of this group is "To Meet Me." The poet, "I," travels to meet the "Me" created by his words. They are both called by the first person singular, but their births, their concerns and their outlooks are not the same. They know their differences are subtle yet irreconcilable, and their differences frustrate both. Yet at the end of the day they are kin to each other, and sleep side by side, becoming "the sparkling dust of the universe." Here we have the poet Tanikawa and his creation the Poet as two separate entities meeting each other face to face, ultimately dispersing their differences and becoming part of the cosmic depths.

The last piece in the group, "I am me, myself" presents a being in the first person singular as an anonymous and amorphous omnipresence. "I" might be the poet himself. Or "I" might be his creation who can hang in thin air, affecting everything around him, including his readers. This ambiguity is the charm of the poem. There is no right or wrong answer, but the uncertainty or ambivalence is significant in itself.

The twelve boys individually presented in the 12-poem series titled "The Boy" are of different ages and from different times. Yet they all display both childlike innocence and seasoned wisdom. When I asked what sort of images Tanikawa has of these youths, he softly said, "The Boy is the boy inside me." So the boys we meet are images from a prism located at the center of his mind, projected in different angles, at various times.

The book ends with "Immortality." At the very end we see a child sitting under a tree, "Smiling softly / for us who are growing old." This suggests the enlightened Buddha, taking the form of an innocent child, watching over us all. Here we have a hint of a warm peaceful communion with the greater presence. We sense an implicit trust and acceptance of spirituality at the core of the universe. What an evolution from his youthful voice, facing the infinite expanse of the universe, "who sneezed in spite of" himself!

In 2009 Tanikawa published a volume of long narrative poems titled *Tromsф Collage* (p. 231). These poems are varied in nature, ranging from an impressionistic soliloquy to an allegory to a drama. "Poet's Tomb" is reprinted in this book together with "An Epitaph to Poet's Tomb." "Ferry to Death" is a dying man's ferry-ride across the river that separates life from the other world. In spite of the gravity of the theme, the poem is surprisingly light-hearted, as if to say death is simply a next step. "This Weaving" is a poetic drama of film artists presented in a manner reminiscent of a radio drama, a film, or a combination of both. Tanikawa successfully converts his technical expertise in other art forms into poetry. A script writer, a director, his wife, and an omniscient voice weave the story of a frustrated artist's intent "to create a space in one's mind where there is not a single soul." Each voice presents a different point of view.

At the beginning of his career, Tanikawa's youthful mind looked out into the infinity of the Cosmos all alone. Over the years, he has tested his aloneness, his art, steadily changing his focus, shifting his sight from the Cosmos to this world, to people, and then to himself. But as *Watashi* (*I Myself*) shows us, all the elements he has accumulated over the years are still inside him, each waiting to be projected onto his poetry. In his newest book of narrative poems, *Tromsφ Collage*, his eyes are once again turning outward. We look forward to seeing yet another pattern of color appear on his chameleon coat.

ABOUT THIS BOOK

This book, *Tanikawa Shuntarō: The Art of Being Alone, Poems 1952–2009* is intended to reflect the depth and breadth of Tanikawa's poetry from his first book of poetry, published in 1952, through his most recent book in 2009. Five books—*Journey* (1968/95), *Fragments of a Forged Talamaikan Manuscript* (1978), *minimal* (2002), *Poet's Tomb* (2006) and *Watashi* (*I Myself*) (2007)—are translated in full. His eighteen other books are represented by extensive selections, with one additional poem from *Selected Poems of Tanikawa Shuntarō II*. My objective was to provide readers with a broad perspective on his diverse interests, techniques, and styles, as well as an overview of the changing focus of his poetry as it evolved over more than half a century. Poems published before 2000 were translated from the CD-ROM collection *Complete Poems of Tanikawa Shuntarō* (Tokyo: Iwanami, 2000). The CD-ROM contains all of his individual books of poetry up to 2000 as originally published. Poems from books published after 2000 were translated from the original print editions. The poems are organized chronologically, by date of their publication in book form. In the case of *Journey,* which was published in 1968 and re-published in 1995 with two additional poems, at Mr. Tanikawa's suggestion I placed it in sequence as per the original 1968 date.

Two poems, "Grass" and "Death and Flames," were translated by W. S. Merwin based on my preliminary versions. This was done as part of a mutual translation project between Mr. Tanikawa and Mr. Merwin, originally published in the poetry journal *Eureka*, Tokyo, November 1981. All other poems contained here are my own translations. The quotations from Japanese sources in this introduction are also my translations.

A word about translation seems appropriate here. When I translate a poem, I first read it closely, trying to feel its emotional charge, and to understand its connotations and significance. Then I try to express in English what I read in Japanese, paying close attention to the original lines and form. My revisions focus on bringing the English version as close as I can manage to the original cadence, diction, and feeling, taking into account the connotations and implications the English words may carry. In other words, I try to be as faithful as possible to the original.

However, translation by its very nature reflects how the translator reads and interprets the original work. Readers may benefit from consulting more than one translation of a piece to form their own understanding of the poem at hand.

Takako U. Lento, 2010

Poems 1952–2009

Alone in Two Billion Light Years
二十億光年の孤独
(1952)

Spring

Along the cute suburban commuter line
I see white contented homes
pathways inviting for walks

At a station in the middle of vegetable farms
no one gets off or on
Along the cute suburban commuter line
however
I also see the chimney of a nursing home

Under the numerous clouds of a March sky
the train slows down
I trade my momentary fatalism
for the scent of plum blossoms

Along the cute suburban commuter line
everything but Spring is off limits

Prayer

One magnanimous affirmation
originating from the tip of infinite time
is still with us, yet
we try to counter it
with countless proposals
(oh, *homo sapiens,* we are too arrogant, too arrogant)

Haven't we been acquiring knowledge
to clarify the affirmation?
Have we not been carrying on
to rejoice in the affirmation?

My immature mind
(a mere rivet in an elaborate half-broken machine)
trusts only prayer now
(offered by the infinitesimal to the infinite in the universe)

I will pray before I sleep
that people's prayers be fortified
that people feel the earth's loneliness as their own

(every location is a point on earth
every one of us is a human)
I will pray, bearing loneliness

One magnanimous affirmation
originating from the tip of infinite time
is still with us, and

one small prayer
feeble yet resolved to be burning on
in dark gigantic time
flames up, now

Alone in Two Billion Light Years

On this small sphere
humans sleep, wake, work
from time to time want friends on Mars

I don't know what Martians do
on their small sphere
(maybe they sleep'eep, wake'ake, work'ork)
but from time to time they want friends on Earth
that's absolutely for sure

Universal gravitation is
the force of being alone, attracting each other

The universe is warped
that is why all of us seek each other

The universe is growing fast
that is why all of us are uneasy

Standing alone in two billion light years
I sneezed, in spite of myself

Nero   *to a beloved small dog*

Nero
Summer will be here soon
your tongue
your eyes
you taking a nap
they all come back to me so clearly

You knew only two summers
I've already known 18 summers
I recall various summers, some my own, some not
Summer in Maisons Laffitte
Summer in Yodo
Summer at Williamsburg Bridge
Summer at Oran
And I wonder
how many summers humans have known

Nero
Summer will be here again soon
but that is not the summer where you were
it will be another summer
a totally different summer

A new summer will come
and I will come to learn many new things
things beautiful, things ugly, things that cheer me up, things that
    make me sad
and I will ask
what on earth are they?
why on earth?
what on earth should I do?

Nero
you died
you went far away all by yourself so no one would know
Your voice
your touch
even your feelings
come back to me now so clearly

48

But Nero
Summer will soon arrive again
a new infinitely open summer will be here
and
I will still walk on
meeting a new summer, autumn, winter
meeting spring, looking forward to yet another new summer
to learn all new things
and
to answer all of my inquiries by myself

Scalpel

!
At that moment the cosmos converged into a gimlet
and I spurned rarefied metaphysics

modifiers saturate
thoughts evaporate
time decelerates
abstraction retreats
oblivion is obliterated

in a series of lightless flashes
in a soundless drum's fortissimo
materialism pierces to reduce
love etc
to protein molecules

with a white bed and capillaries as my starting point
I reclaimed my ordinary coordinates
then what pained me right away was
knotty discussions on existence

A Walk on a Cloudy Day

<When it is so darkly clouded over
I can't even have a chat with a cloud>

After all, in heavens with no blue sky
there aren't any so-called answers
In heat graced with moisture
I rather yearn for a pickaxe

<Yeah, for a cloud, I prefer a small cumulonimbus
but my memories of the war are still so real, you know?>

Burnt fields have summer grasses
the summer grasses are asserting their own will
I'll ask God
what He thinks of humans

<Nah, I won't despair
I just miss the blue sky>

એ

62 Sonnets
六十二のソネット
(1953)

19 *Vastness*

I walk on
in the vast sea of things
now the wind rises
then Time stirs

Its subtle motion too
will soon be forgotten
In the vast expanse nobody notices
Time dies

I will stay aware of a vastness people can't even imagine
I will be mindful of my life and death
among the things that are indifferent to me

I walk on   as if I were one of those things
I stop looking
Suddenly then I begin to live

30

I do not allow words to rest
Once in a while my words feel embarrassed and
try to die inside me
At that time, I am in love

Among things that do not talk
only people are loquacious
The sun, the trees and the clouds
don't even know how beautiful they are

A swift airplane speeds away in the shape of human passion
The blue sky pretends to be a backdrop, but
nothing is really there

I give a try calling out in a small voice
The Cosmos does not respond
My words are no different from the call of a small bird

41

When I gaze into the blue of the sky
I feel I have a place to return to
but the light that has come through the clouds
no longer returns to the sky

The sun ceaselessly sheds itself in abundance
we are busy gathering it even into night
humans are all of humble birth
so we do not rest in opulence like trees

The window cuts away the overflowing
I do not want a room other than the universe
This makes me at odds with others

To be is to injure space and time
their pain in turn torments me
when I leave here I may be wholesome again

61

My heart touches the Cosmos softly
affirming the shape the Cosmos takes
now the wind rises . . .
now a boy is dashing on . . .

My heart touches itself also
it always returns to
my self inseparable from the Cosmos
in order to sing, if hesitantly —

Who will glean my ode to joy?
Joy deserves to be returned to earth
then it will not rot away all alone

No need for words
about my love
the Cosmos will know it by my gaze alone

62

Because the Cosmos embraces me with love
(heartlessly, or at times
tenderly)
I can be alone for ever

When a woman was granted me for the first time
I was just listening for the resonance of the Cosmos

Only simple sorrows and joys are clear to me
because I always belong to the Cosmos

I throw myself

at the sky, at the tree, at the woman
all soon to be part of abundance of the Cosmos itself

. . . I call to her
then the Cosmos looks back
and I am no more

ଔ

On Love
愛について
(1955)

The Sky's Deceit

Birds fly happily because the sky is there
the sky is happy being there because birds fly in it
When a man looks up at the sky all alone
who will do anything to make him happy?

Airplanes expose the back side of the sky
as if to shame the sky
When a man sees what the sky is all about
he annihilates it
After a plane cuts into the sky and injures it
birds heal it with their gentle wings
The birds are not aware that the sky is deceitful
because of that the sky is there for those birds

<The sky is blue   but there is nothing to the sky>
<There is nothing in the sky   and thanks to that birds can fly in
   the sky>

Birds

Birds do not name the sky
birds simply fly in the sky
birds do not name insects
birds simply eat insects
birds do not name love
birds simply live as mates

birds know how to sing
that is why birds do not notice the world
suddenly a gunshot is heard
a small lump of lead separates the bird from the world and
  connects it to Man
and Man's colossal lies become a humble truth inside the bird

Man believes in the bird for a moment
but even then Man does not believe in the sky
that is why Man is not aware of the colossal lies that tie the bird,
  the sky and himself
Man is always left ignorant
soon, in death, made into a bird for the sky
he finally comes to know the colossal lies, to learn that the lies
  are the truth

Birds do not name life
birds are simply moving
birds do not name death
they simply stop moving

the sky simply spreads out for ever

Notes   *to John Cage*

Notes flow,
they do not wish to be a river, but
they somehow disappear and
there it is, a river flowing

The notes first meant to be a new river, but
at times were too fast, or too slow
to be a river
The river of notes would allow clouds to be reflected too

and people would look back at them
and even run alongside the river keeping pace with them
But as trees on its riverbank give forth fresh leaves
people would realize that the river of notes has no Spring or Fall
But as the notes forget what they might become
flowing on, so totally exposed
fatigued by folly and humility
they now are a river and
they are not even aware that they are a river
As they throw themselves open
as if to say they don't care what they are
don't care if they are not notes or a river
somehow Spring arrives, and Summer comes
they don't even know they are now trees

The notes do not look at themselves
they breathe inside what make them come alive
The notes no longer make people dance
nor make people cry
They get mixed in with the world
they keep on singing as eternally as the lunar cycle
they are among people as stealthily as the lunar cycle

. . . in this way the notes take their leave

Billy the Kid

fine dirt first lands on my lips, then come larger and larger lumps of dirt onto my belly, between my legs. an ant, its nest gone, briefly walks across my closed eyelids. People have stopped crying now and seem to be feeling good about wielding shovels and sweating. in my chest are two holes shot there by the gentle-eyed sheriff. my blood gushed instantly from these two escape routes. then for the first time it was clear to me that this blood was not mine. I knew my blood was going home and I along with it. above me is my only enemy the dry blue sky. it has consumed me totally, while running, shooting, even making love, that blue sky has consumed me. but the only time it fails to consume me is when I die. now I will not be consumed. for the first time I have no fear of the blue sky. I am not afraid of that silence that fathomless blue. because now the earth is going to consume me. I can now go home to where the blue sky can no longer reach me. to where I don't have to fight. it is now that my voice will be answered. it is now that the sound of my gunshots will stay in my ears now that I can no longer hear or shoot

by killing I tried to test men and myself. the color of blood decorated my youthful means of proof

but I cannot paint over the blue sky with someone else's blood. I sought my own blood. today I got it. I proved that my blood darkened the blue sky and then returned to the earth. now I no longer see the blue sky or remember it. I smell my own earth now waiting for me to become the earth. the wind flows over me. I am not jealous of the wind any more. soon I will be the wind. soon I will live in the blue sky not knowing the blue sky. I will become a single star. I will be a star that knows all nights, knows the height of all days and cycles on

Menstruation

1

Inside a woman someone prepares a feast for a ritual. Inside a woman someone sculpts a son yet unknown. Inside a woman someone is wounded.

2

God's palm
wounded clumsily in creation, still unable to forget it even now.

3

<With such regularity, florid funeral rites are held inside me. For those mourned with the color of festivity, for those returning to nothingness unable to be wounded or die.

My children too immature . . .
The ripe moon comes falling. No one catches it.

I wait. Squatting alone in a cold place I wait for a seed to be sown on the moon, for the risen tide to be drained away, unable to heal my inner wound no longer clear whose memory it was>

4

. . . Luring toward the shore what is hoping to live, the tide rises inside a woman. The sea is inside a woman.

As the moon calls, as the moon cycles, there is a never-ending calendar inside a woman.

A Chair

Like a large bird shot down, she is lying flat. Her arms, like wings no longer useful, are bent by her cheeks. She is lying on the bed stark naked. In her semi-sleep, now, she hears a man open the door and leave, which is not accompanied with that silence after the door closes when *he* leaves, with that feeling of dilution, with that feeling as if something is voided out of her. That is because the man who just left is not *him*. That's why she does not awake. That silence would certainly wake her up. But now she is sleepy, because that man is not *him*. . . . She dreams. A very brief dream. *He* is standing by the bed.   *He* is getting smaller and smaller. Then something gets caught in her throat. She tries to cough it out but it is hard to get it out. That is *him*. She cannot stop coughing. She drinks a decoction. Its steam turns into *him* this time. Then *he* turns into humidity to make her feel oppressed. Footsteps pass by outside the window. They are from the man who just left. Somehow his steps are not orderly as if he is walking on four legs. His legs were hard and thin. Come to think of it, his arms, too. She wakes up to clarity, but not her body yet. What did the man say at the beginning? "It's a bit cold." Five minutes or so later, "Would you warm me up?" She had almost fallen asleep already. . . .

But is it morning already? Trains are moving in a distance. Inside her head is a corner of a town in early morning. Cold and foggy, and the shoes sound strangely crisp. The sun has not risen yet. Suddenly, her ankles itch. She thinks of scratching there, but her hands are lazy and will not follow her will. She says under her breath, "I may be with child." And she tries to voice, "child . . ." then falls asleep again.

The sun rises. The sun rises from somewhere around the right shoulder of the life insurance company at the corner of the fifth street. The blue sky is not blue. The shutters of her room let in light from their left top corner. At first the dust at the corner of her desk looms up. The light beams reach her eyes next. The soft downy hair on her eyelids begins to shine. *He* is looking at it in silence. He is just standing carrying a large briefcase. She is not awake yet. He is counting seconds in his mind. It is already about time everyone is at the office. At that moment she opens her eyes. She asks, "When did you come?" As always he answers, "Now, just now." And absently he says what he noticed, "The chair is gone, isn't it?" Instead of answering, she says, with her eyes narrowed as if to avoid glare, "I may be with child." Unconsciously moving his hand that is not holding the briefcase as if to punch a time clock, he thinks for a moment, "Need a wet nurse." That moment he senses the vacuous room throwing a quick glance at him.

A Room

He fenced himself in because
space was so fearsome and
time was so sorrowful

This makes me secure, he thought
He had pure white walls in place of infinite space
He had a comfortable bed in place of infinite time

But he needed a door and a window
The door was for his close friends
The window was for the beautiful summer's day

In the daytime the outside also had walls such as the blue sky
    and cumulonimbus clouds
It had beds like fields and a town
But at night he closed himself in

"The room brings back fond memories," so he always mumbled
The room faithfully let him live in a familiar frame of reference
Through Spring, Summer, Fall, Winter, and until his death one day

I don't know what happened to him after that
Without him the room
grew more and more like the universe

ଓଃ

21
(1962)

Perusal

     a

I see a woman
looking this way from under her large summer hat

I see a dogwood tree behind her
I see knots on its trunk

A kid's bike speeds past
fountain water is falling

I see everything that refuses to halt
a bronze statue is being demolished

I see ants at my feet
I see a dead ant that the ants are carrying

I see a hand held out to me
I see the sunlight through leaves dancing on the hand and

tarot cards spread open I see
my resplendent victory

     b

I see a woman
She is my grandmother

I see the gigantic clear eyes
of reptiles long extinct

I see a lateen sail sway in the ocean current
as a sailing ship sinks into the sea

The Imperial Guards line up at attention
I see their singing skeletons

I see a rocky hill plowed
I see the same hill burnt and scalded

Blood rushes to cheeks
Flesh opens up

Among the crowds at a Festival
I see Medusa's severed head

C

I see a woman
She once was my love

A heart pulsates
on a balance that is swaying

The shrieking of a newspaper seller
courses through the streets

I see infinite faces in the world
which I was not able to capture

films are fading
a choo-choo train is running after a horse

Various species of angels are impaled on insect pins
Martini glasses are raised for a toast

A record is playing
I see a delicate scar on the record

d

I see a woman
I see my wife

I see tears slowly welling up
I see translucent milk squeezed out

I see a broad back
a cotton ball being torn

a firm ripe fruit and
an artless drawing of the fruit

I see all that I have thoroughly looked at
I see myself refusing to look at it again

A long polished hallway
slithers away like a snake

I see lips suddenly coming at me
in a hot shower

e

I see a woman
She is my daughter

I see her belly button shaped like a question mark
I see idle light caught in the fine hair on her earlobe

Caught in the folds of a loose robe
I cannot arrive at dawn

I see blood oozing over it
recovery being denied

the thick layer of dust on the Moon's surface and
the lakes all dried up

an open forehead offered to the sky
a love like a thrown pebble

I see what I am not allowed to see
in a pensive look on her gentle face

f

I see a woman
my mother

an empty urn as blue as the sky
outside the windowpane

I see a sheet of music laid open and
candlelight illuminating harmonic chords

a broken pearl necklace and
an icicle hanging from the water pipe

I see a toddler being whipped
a blackboard that cannot be erased

ocean water brims over
in numerous verses

I see my father crying and screaming in the dark
I see myself being born

g

I see a woman
That is me

I see a face being placed over another face
I see a hidden passage of flesh

Images that are patched together in the depth of a mind
Witty words that forever aspire to but never achieve perfection

A mold of buttocks that stays forever warm
on an old large bed

A heated towel forgotten
in a path between boulders

I see a kitchen, shining, with no one around
A book that has never been read

I see a shaman in a trance
behind a shabby blanket

Ad lib of the day

Whiskers

whiskers grow
whiskers grow on men's chins around their lips whiskers grow
   with the dawn whiskers grow like shoots of some strange plant
   whiskers grow for women's tender cheeks whiskers grow like
   Salvador Dali's whiskers grow with all their might whiskers
   grow facing the sun whiskers grow on men
but
they shave every morning they shave worrying about bus
   schedules they shave the razors are Gillette Valette they shave
   terrified of women's caresses they shave while bleeding they
   shave
from sideburn to jaw a dead fish slides inside a mirror
they shave
their jowls are blue ocean they shave for Cannes High Society
   they shave for Monaco boredom army cadets shave like the
   greens on a golf course swindlers shave widowers shave
   citizens shave
Don't!
Grow a beard!
like cactus in Texas
grow a beard like Castro grow a beard like Lincoln to seek the
   freedom of growing a beard grow a beard yearning to be a
   monk grow a beard for women lion cubs grow beards our dear
   King of Hades grows a beard naturally fully naturally grow a
   beard and men make speeches

Nellie

I'm pregnant. I sit by the window pane, pregnant. I am a yellow, white and brown woman. I'm pregnant. My soul, boob-shaped, hangs over y'all men's tongues. It's already six now. Too late to pray. Rain is running down the window pane. Potted geraniums bloom. Somewhere an operation has begun. I hear scalpels touching one another. Come on in. Come into my room and groan. Groan in a guy's voice, in a bass like guys' ground water. My heart ditched geometry a long time ago.

Words ditched poetry a long time ago. Even so you guys should be silent. Groan! I'm listening to you. Why? 'Cause I'm pregnant. 'Cause I'm carrying you. My belly button opens and breathes in slowly. That's all right. Just go ahead and groan. Go right ahead.

Marijuana

Sweat smarts in my eyes
Blood collects in my finger tips
Slobber at my lips
sax' sex babbling saliva's success
agitating every rhythm pursuing a single heart
an image is being sought
an image of an old broken banjo
an image of a spear cutting through the sky
an image of a sun-dial in Venice
an image of the Virgin walking away
an image of a door with flaking varnish
an image of Christopher Columbus
an image of the sea grandly undulating
an image of history bleeding
an image of fifteen cups of coffee
I look for my face in them
I look for love in them

Gigantic roots are growing wild
I don't know where they are bound for
From the tips of branches to be born and to die above ground
uncountable corpses hang
soon to fall to the ground
below them are the gigantic roots growing wild

COOL

It's cold here.
It's cold here, Miles.
I've got a wife and kids, yet
it's cold, Miles.
You are a cool negro, Miles.
Don't leave me behind
Don't give up on our civilization
It's cold here, Miles, and
you are cool.
Your murmur through your thick lips is cool
cooler than any abstract art in a New York gallery
It is cooler than a stuck-up French fashion model's kiss
Ah, modern living!
It's cold here
Though I own stocks, a car and a cottage
it's cold here
You are a cool negro, Miles
you disgrace us with your pink blood
you slap us softly with the fair inside of your hand
I've got Bach and Rembrandt but
you were born out of Bongo's womb
brought up at the blue canal bottom of the blues
you tell your own fortune with cards in a whorehouse in Harlem
and you stare straight at me
It's cold here

I've had enough of your gentle mute
Blow through me, Miles, instead of your 'pet
Warm me with your breaths, soak me
I'm going to ditch
my woman blond all over in an elevator
Mark my penthouse on your black new map. . . .

You are a cool negro, Miles
I will lynch you
It's not cold here
I've got everything!

A Village of Poets

A Room of Silence

It is surrounded by four plaster walls. The walls look fresh as if they were just painted, but in fact they were painted centuries ago. However, the residents here have never brought in any furniture, and even their breathing has been so quiet from time to time (of course they did not even dream of using fire) the white walls have never been stained or darkened by soot, looking fresh forever. On one of the plaster walls, (Why am I so vague as to say "one"? Because there is no window here to orient myself) a door is hung. This door is merely a picture, an extremely realistic painting. In other words, even if one opens this door, one will only see a white plaster wall. But the ceiling is very high. It's tall, and narrowed toward the top, like the inside of a steep four cornered pyramid. It is so extremely narrow at the top that one would need a hairpin to clean it. The ceiling is plastered white like the walls, and of course not a single speck of dust or stain is there.

The floor is made of stone. Granite directly connected to the earth's crust was polished flat. To be precise, though, one cannot call it flat any longer. Many people's feet (in wooden clogs, in straw slippers, in spiked shoes, or in bare feet) have worn down the floor over many centuries. The middle of the floor is the most worn and depressed. This is proof that many of the people desired to be in the center of the room, and if carefully observed, bloodstains are there even though quite minuscule.

Unfamiliar Poem-Man

I saw a tall man. The tall man was thin and stark naked. His skin was full of wrinkles like elephant skin, and his penis pointed to the earth like an arrow mark. His face had no eyes, but had two walnuts instead. He seemed to see trees and rocks and women with them. His gaze tasted something like dry wind, and I drank his gaze up, standing between him and the woods. The tall man said, "To tell you the truth, I am Poem-Man," in a voice low and seemingly tired. When the tall man turned around, I saw writing crowded all over his gray back. The letters seemed to be all small puncture wounds, but I could not decipher them. All I could do was to lick with my tongue a bit of blood oozing out of a few still-fresh letters trailing toward his buttocks.

Poem-Eye

I rubbed the surface of my wife's rounded belly with poetry, and polished her up with licorice-scented poetry. Then, for some reason, my wife became extremely thin. But thanks to that she became as beautiful as a superbly polished line of poetry. My wife was desperately trying to tell me something, but by that time her mouth was full of the straw and water I had stuffed there. All I could hear was some meaningless moan.

But as I was looking at her waxy nude body, I suddenly sensed changes in my eyes. My pupils were dilated to match those of the dead, and my crystalline lens focused on infinity. I got it instantly: I was seeing everything with the gaze of a poem, that is, Poem-Eye! I no longer had any reason to rub her with poetry. My wife quickly grew rounded, with her skin darkened like a shark's. So what? Every night I embraced my wife tight in my arms. She bore me children one after another. I tied them, one after another, to a willow tree, and used a whip to train each carefully for every acrobatic feat.

Poem-Eye! Love and tenderness, and laughable obligations!
Thus I wound up joining in worldly word games.

❧

Journey
旅
(1968)

Toba 1

I have nothing to write about
My flesh is bared to the sun
My wife is beautiful
My children are healthy

Let me tell you the truth
I am not a poet
I just pretend to be one

I was created, and left here
Look, the sun cascades among the boulders
making the sea look darker

Other than this quiet at the height of the day
I have nothing I want to tell you about
even if you are bleeding in your country
Ah, this everlasting radiance!

Toba 2

I don't want to make this moment eternal
It is fine to own this moment just as it is
Even I have a way to seize a transient moment
The sun is already moving on

These words are merely
written on the sand
not with my fingers
but with my cheerful heart that shifts quickly to gloom

My children look like me
My children don't look like me
Either way it pleases me

Along with sea shells, pebbles and pieces of broken bottles
my heart is left at the water's edge of a planet
just as hard and vulnerable

Toba 3

The old woman is looking at the sand as she gathers brushwood
I am looking at the horizon from my hotel window
You, who have lived through hunger,
please go ahead and torture me

I have always lived with my belly full
Even now I am belching
The least I can wish is to deserve your hatred

Old woman, what could my words do for you?
I do not wish to atone for anything any more
What strangles me is what you have in your hand
the horizon you will not look at

I hear Clementi's sonatina faintly
No one speaks to me
What deep comfort

Toba 4

With my own saliva caught in my windpipe
I choke and cough for quite a while
I wonder if one could die from this

Something words cannot catch in advance
sneaks into my heart from the ocean
My big book of poetry turns to ashes

I gaze at the boulders before my eyes
I gaze at pine trees
I cling to gazing
with no desire for any expression

There's no poetry
no music, but
a single rhythm appears in my heart and
tears are coming to my eyes

Toba 5

I wrote them —
those lame words —
how do they fit which part of me?

I know what I cannot express in words
I don't know what I did express.
A boat is coming back from the sea
I cannot see its oarsman

Words do not ride in the wind
Words do not appear on paper

They do not come to me
I will no longer ask questions
but only answer to my own being
If there is any bitterness leveled against me
that is silence, nothing else

Toba 6

Sea —
even this single word contains deceit
But I insist on saying it
facing the waves rising before a storm

Sea! . . .
then I am left speechless
Into this darkness, my wife,
stretch out your suntanned arms

Your body needs no metaphors
a mouth sealing a mouth
scentless sweat sliding

But we groan
The groan is now a sweet murmur
to my heated ear, closer than the sea

Toba 7

With my sulky mouth shut
again I am unjust to words
As my punishment
I hear the ocean tide through the night

I write:
all poetry is empty words
and I continue on writing

My child wakes up suddenly in the middle of the night
she sobs quite a while
I want to be honest

Even a dying soldier is not honest
My cigarette ashes fall on my lap
I will not dream now
though I am so sleepy

Toba 8

By the time the day is bright
it will be clear that this is not a good poem
but I cannot erase my own words

When people gather at the market
I drink a glass of water at the table
and do nothing else

A white statue stands
by the pool far beyond tree branches
That is me
with my bare testicles open to everyone's eyes

After copying over and over
I have grown to be
a piece of stone
so totally unlike Orpheus

Toba 9

Gently —
however gently I walk I still make sound
on this very thick carpet

This is also a message from somebody
a whisper one can hardly call a whisper
and this sound is also a word

Even screeching machinery never deafened me
but now
I cover my ears tightly
with both my hands

Then even more loudly
I hear human blood coursing through me
I hear a voice speaking to me
the voice so infinitely tranquil

Toba 10

The morning we are to leave
I hear a local dialect or two
mixed in with my family's endless chatter

The wind rises from inside me
Toba is already a vast desolation
Even a piece of stale cake
is owing to some sacrifice

I want to recall
a line in a poem I left incomplete and forgot

Jealous for even one word
I patiently wait for the incarnation of words
The sun shoots into my eyes
The ceaseless winds sing through pine trees
There is no copybook for me to follow

Toba Addendum

Just now Inspiration ran past me
leaving me with a meager number of words
not to convey something
the words are writhing like infants

A journey to words
is as far and uncertain as a journey to Mars
A vacuous profound rumble
is apt to engulf me

And thrown at me for the first time
are the words from you of bleached bones
They are
. . . .
I cannot come up with them

Trip I

On a pretty picture postcard
I have nothing to write
I am here, now

The iced coffee is good
The strawberry pastry is tasty
What was the name of the river flowing through the town

so remarkably gently?
I am here, now
I just don't feel it is real
Because I am really here
I would be able to talk about it
as a recollection, but
now, in this place
I simply am

Trip 2

A gypsy
banged on my car window and yelled
There was not even an incommunicable word
in Ostia

Dirt walls buried in dirt
Dried up wells
Pine cones

That place is here
here, not some other place
here for the gypsy, here for me
I am here

There is no escaping
His hands have already touched
even the blue sky

Trip 3

Arizona

The road stretches straight to the horizon
It is painful to feel nothing

I look back
to see the road coming straight at me from the horizon

I could not tell if the scenery was large or small
It was mirrored in my eyes
and that was simply that

Was that the world?
Was it me?
It is silent now too

And now I —
I no longer care what I am
My words get in the way
of reaching the center of silence

Trip 4
Alicante

I see a picture post card
I see Time
this is not a memory
this is not now

My mind is transparent
I see the ocean on the other side of my mind
neither dark nor radiant

Do not intervene,
Words,
between the ocean and me

On my temple
a drop of sweat appears

How clear-cut
the place name is

Trip 5

Round coins, large and small,
constantly jingle in my pocket
Thank you is spoken
at a rapid pace in every country

I arrived here, tired out, but
how close everything is
everywhere

I favor my wife and child over
Madonna and Child statues all around
The horsy faces of Romanesque statues
The skin and bones of Gothic statues

I touch the chair I am sitting on
Its cast iron is faintly warm
Right now, I have nothing to spare in my heart

Trip 6

Oahu

As it fades
it becomes ever more clear
while it is clear
it is already almost gone

The rainbow hangs over a town
and it's nowhere to be seen

sugar canes sway in the wind
as far as the eyes can reach

This present moment torments me deep in my heart
Is it because there is no need for words,
or is it because words fail me?

Visible as it disappears,
visible already
only in my thoughts

Trip 7

The rocks are in harmony with the sky
It is Poetry
I cannot write it

There is no way to reach words
by working on silence
I will try to arrive at this silence
by polishing words

The tree is shaped like a tree
singing in the wind
It does not matter where it stands

If I feel just as I see
all would glow in beauty
If I write like I see
time would cease

Trip 8

A single young tree is hiding the setting sun
I am standing in its long shadow
The scenery is complete on its own, no need for metaphors
Gap-toothed man with hunched shoulders,
tending a donkey —
you know how I failed to write when I tried

Words come to serve you,
a man of few words,
The air is plentiful
The quiet spreads into infinity

A thistle butterfly flutters down
All these will
stay on
after I die

anonym I

If I stay silent
I must say I am silent
If I cannot write
I must write that I cannot write

That's the spirit
However drained I feel
I am a man
not by virtue of a single tree
not by virtue of a single bird
only by virtue of a single word

I do not hope to have you give me an answer
You can simply lean on a chair
You can simply rely on the mass of men

But I will give my own answer
to the light that is about to dissolve into the woods
to the scream I could not hear, to silence

anonym 2

Mommy! —
Was that my kid?
Or someone else's?

It sounded so terrified
What can I do for you?
You would grasp the whole
while I can show you only a fraction

You kept running on
not crying
Which way did you go?

The single scream
I can no longer locate it —
will another kid decipher it?
someday?

anonym 3

to Takemitsu Tōru

At the corner of a large white sheet of music
notes begin to gather

like mosquito larvae
From the closed cave
in the depth of your chest
breath comes out
to mix with the Spring air

This moment reaches everyone's ears,
though no one tries to listen:
lace curtains sway in the wind
children are loud . . .

At a corner of a large white silence
sounds begin to gather
like nebulae   distantly

anonym 4

The afternoon sun casts its light
on the corpse of a cat that was just run over
Its soul could have chosen to stay with him for life
if it wanted to

But it passes on in an instant
silently
leaving so much behind

No matter how small a thing is
it cannot be fully elaborated
Silence contains
just words

The edges of clouds shine in gold
Music
seduces me

anonym 5

White — beyond the bird like a pebble
backdrop of growing clouds
I desire so earnestly to live
yet today I feel it all right to die

What declaration do I need?
Beyond my eroding mind
far, far away
there's that something, limitless
A murmur . . .
not worth recording in words
not worth singing about

In that murmur
already dwells a gentle resolve
a resolve that will never lead to action

anonym 6

it's like a scent
it's right here, but no longer here
it's not here, but brimming over
like Time

there's a brick wall
it's on the wall, but won't let you grab it
it's something you couldn't possibly name
like Light

a gadfly in the light
the buzz of its wings
the sound of those things —

like
something like
that

anonym 7

I wrote yesterday
yet I no longer remember how to write a poem
I am a middle-aged man with no skill in my hands
even though lust is still with me

What should I start with,
chattering voices outside my fence,
the window panes shaken by the wind,
my breath?

The cosmos is silent
as long as I remain silent
This momentary equilibrium —

With my elbows on my desk
with my eyes staring at the wall
I am a Sphinx . . .

anonym 8

Breaths become turbulent thoughts
Thoughts turn into heavy sighs
Sighs change into hushed murmurs
Murmurs suddenly explode into screams

Yet ultimately words are undefined
The screams become a silent deed

The deed is forever watched by Death
That somehow brings about songs
The songs once again return
to the tangled breaths of the multitude

The silence inside their breaths is
the angry cries of falling leaves, the wailing of the blue sky
howls from piles and piles of corpses

છ

A Pensive Youth
うつむく青年
(1971)

Can You Hear?

How about being silent?
just a bit of time would do
how about staying silent,
newspapers, radios and you, too
(and also poets)?

Can you hear the quiet
that lurks between lovers at dusk?
Can you hear that quiet
in the gentle eyes of a deer looking at you
can you hear the quiet
the sky is always secretly hiding?

Quietly
so quietly as to not deafen the quiet
can you say a good morning and a good night?

The Sea

beneath the cloud whorl
the undulating skin of the planet

at times violently snaps
a gigantic tanker like a twig
at times allows a small dugout
to drift gently

the yet-to-be-developed
negative of Land

tying patterns together
separating God from gods
shutting in islands
transporting slaves

the weightiest blue
breaks into shimmering white

it provides a net full of fish
for a poor fisherman
a single line of horizon
for a dreaming youth

the tumult from pre-genesis
surging over and over toward the other shore

The sea!

The New Frontier — Apollo I I —

No flowers will be there
No seeds either
No breeze will be there
No loose locks on a nape either
No small birds will be there
No plankton either
Just a man
A single man is standing
In the new wilderness

(Fragile flesh encased in a bulky space suit)

But
Dreams will be there
Prejudices, too
Courage will be there
Fear, too
Countless words will be there
(Oh, not yet familiar God!)
Silence, too
Because it is a man
Because of a single man
in a new frontier

☙

The Day Small Birds Vanished from the Sky

空に小鳥がいなくなった日
(1974)

Morning

It is morning again, and I am alive
Totally forgetting my dreams overnight I see
the bare branches of the persimmon tree sway in the wind
I see a dog, with no collar, lie in a pocket of sunlight

I was not here one hundred years ago
I will not be here one hundred years from now
The earth must be a place beyond our imaginations
though it seems so ordinary

Once upon a time inside a womb
I was a tiny tiny egg
Then I came to be a tiny tiny fish
Then I came to be a tiny tiny bird

Then finally I came to be human
having lived hundreds of billions of years in nine months
We need to revisit that, too
because we've only been looking ahead too much

The cold clarity of a drop of water this morning
tells me what a human is
I want to share this water
with fish, with birds and
even with beasts that might kill me

A Morning Takes Shape

What has tormented my mind since last evening
appeared in a dream like an endless barren land
Somewhere in the dream my alarm clock rang
My dog was wagging his tail beyond the glass doors
The sunlight shot sideways at a glass on the table
There it was, it was morning

The morning was bright that day, too.
Its light bared me to all the corners of my soul
frighteningly clearly
I could no longer fool myself
I said, "Good morning!"
I felt the words keep me from harm

The morning was there
Cold water rushed out of the faucet
The smell of *miso* soup filled the room
People were intent on walking in all the walks of the country
I saw the morning take shape
surer than happiness, brighter than hope

Inside Myself

Inside myself
is a profound cry
that makes my mouth shut up tight

Inside myself
is a night that will not end
that makes my eyes open wide

Inside myself
is a stone that goes rolling on
that causes my feet to stand still
Inside myself
is a circuit that is closed
that causes my mind to open

Inside myself
is something no metaphor could express
that causes my words to be written down

Inside myself
yes, inside my own being
are flesh and blood that bind me to you

That causes a man to be so alone like this
separate from another

The Day Small Birds Vanished from the Sky

The day beasts vanished from the wood
the wood held its breath in silence
The day beasts vanished from the wood
humans kept building their roads

The day fish vanished from the sea
the sea absently undulated and groaned
The day fish vanished from the sea
humans kept building their ports

The day children vanished from town
the town was ever more bustling
The day children vanished from town

humans kept building their parks
The day humans lost their inner selves
they looked very much like each other
The day humans lost their inner selves
humans kept believing in their future

The day small birds vanished from the sky
the sky wept silently
The day small birds vanished from the sky
humans kept singing unawares

☙

At Midnight in the Kitchen I Wanted to Talk to You
夜中に台所でぼくはきみに話しかけたかった
(1975)

Grass

and all at once
one time
out of some place
I was standing in this grass
All I have to do
was recorded in my cells
That is why I took the shape of a man
and even talked about happiness
>   (*translated by W. S. Merwin with Takako Lento*)

At Midnight in the Kitchen I Wanted to Talk to You

1

Two junior high kids, a boy and a girl,
are sitting on a subway bench, you see,
Cheshire cat smiles pasted on their faces
they are chatting, showing peach colored gums

In comes a subway train, gwaooh-gwaooh,
I'd have thought they'd get on it, but they don't, you know

gwaooh-gwaooh, off goes the train
that's the context of this line in our times

Why don't you guys just do it, get it over with?
I'm too involved with myself
to watch over you
until you guys get to be my age

2   *to Takemitsu Tōru*

I bet you are drinking tonight too, somewhere
I hear ice clink in your glass
You'd talk a lot, and then fall silent with no warning
Even though the cause of our pain is one
we have different ways of diversion
Do you beat your wife?

3   *to Oda Minoru*

It's no use accusing just the prime minister
He isn't even a symbol
your Osaka dialect is eternal
but prime ministers change in short order

There's a stream in the refrigerator, you know,
I am drinking coffee in my kitchen
Justice is not my cup of tea
so at least I will make my handwriting steady

Then tomorrow will come
tomorrow, so snugly fitted into history,
yet sticking out of it
with mysterious arrogance
Shall I say good morning while it's still night?

4   to Tanikawa Tomoko

I don't blame you for getting angry
I am telling you to love me at my ugliest
what's more, while sober

I am in an absolute bind
I probably need a catharsis
like that of Oedipus
provided, of course, I can survive that
without losing my eyesight

I wonder what the chorus would sing for me?
I bet they'd clamor in unison
something about an Oedipus complex and such

They've got a point
Interpretation is always a step behind, but
to be honest, what I'd really prefer to get is
an utterly unreasonable oracle

5

I've done enough yapping like a know-it-all
No more chatter to the printing machines
I want someone facing me — I don't care if it's a ghost
though it'll annoy me if I get talked to

It would be good if money turned into tree leaves
not all, but just about half of it
then I could sit spaced-out all day long
gazing at the tree leaves

It will be nice to have lightning come closer from the distance
then to have rain arrive

It may even be ok to have a burglar break into my house
surely better than legal statements

Suppose a ghost grows younger and younger
and reverts to, say, a beautiful Oiwa before poison disfigured her
I wonder if I can make her happy

6

Being totally silent, that's pretty good, isn't it?
a guy like a cymbal in an orchestra, you see
he shouts to his limit, just once, or maybe twice
and then he sits back for the rest of the time
what to do while just sitting?
keeping bees might be good
then, the theme of his shouting would be bees

Though bees are his theme, naturally
he ends up talking about life
even if he just screeches
tonal qualities are totally different, you see
how do I put it? his vocal cords, his Adam's apple, and his tongue
all, I think, have grown quite thick
yet they are not tough, you know

his spit sprays out, too

7

I will send you a post card
The card will say something like I'm fine and such
but that's not it, to be precise
To say I'm not fine is not right either,
the truth is somewhere in between
in other words, it's normal, but that is something inscrutable

Being normal is a balanced state between massive despair like
     silk floss and
a minuscule amount of hope like lead
like a zoo on Sundays, for example,
teeming with monkeys and humans

Anyhow I will write you a card
the card will say I am fine
though, after a glass of cola,
I am no longer certain
which of us is on a trip, you or I

My best

8   to Iijima Kōichi

On the spur of the moment, I wrote a few pieces of
something like poetry, grabbing this style for now
You say you are in bed, depressed
I am still up and around, depressed
I don't know what to do, so I am up and writing
Since I am writing, maybe I am not depressed?
But everything seems pointless
I've even come to hate Mozart, you see
I wish I could at least touch something
something like a well-crafted box of unvarnished wood
If I can touch it, then I will want to caress it
If I can caress it, then I will want to grab it
If I can grab it, I may well smash it
What about you?
How are your fingers doing?
Your thumbs are still thumbs?
Can you wipe yourself clean after you poop?
My poor fellow, you

9

It doesn't matter what the title is
Titling a poem is snobbish
I am a snob, of course, but
I simply have no time for a title now

If I do, I will call it "All"
If not, I'll use something like, that's about it for now
Azaleas are blooming in my yard
They are beautiful
because they are mindlessly blossoming
Even so, azaleas won't do for a title, will it?
Even while I am writing about azaleas
other things pop up in my head
terrible Japanese words are plentiful
wouldn't it be nice if azaleas alone were free of them all?

one's got only one soul, that's why

10   after Charlie Brown

My old shoes were by my bed, you see
that's why I felt like getting up again this morning
Time is really like a clock, isn't it?
It doesn't get tired or anything, it just keeps working

Let's change the subject

Wind is blowing over the weeds
I turn my eyes to the familiar sight once again

Not easy to change the subject, is it?

11

If, suddenly, a total stranger, barfing,
falls into your arms
can you hold him up,
I mean, before you wipe his puke off your shirt?

I'd probably hold him up, but
the moment I did that,
I'd look at myself holding him up
in a picture frame
to critique it before others do

I'd puke at the stink of his puke,
but that would be after I get home
that is worse than hypocrisy, isn't it?

Bringing up such an example is
in itself so disgusting, you'd say
but I've already written it

What are you going to do about it?

12

My pencil fell on the floor and made a terrible noise
My wife rolled over in bed
I am writing things like this
because I have lost my past
I get dizzy when I look back into the past
'cause humans think so many different things
to be honest I couldn't care less
yet I can't come up with even a single thought of my own
I feel as if I am the noise the pencil made, falling
kerplunk, plunk, plunk . . .

this sound, with no past, has no future, either
Well —
there's no continuing along this line, is there?

13   to Yuasa Jōji

The fountain at Hibiya Park was lit up in rainbow colors
a man stood in the middle of it
showered by splashes he stood with his arms wide open
a crowd gathered around, and applauded
the wind was still very chilly

I was listening to a folk concert
at the open-air theater until the sunset
a number of paper planes were flying, — and crashing
banjos were resonant
tree tops were swaying in the wind and plenty of similar songs

Music spoils me, and music saves me
Music saves me and music spoils me

14   to Kanaseki Hisao

"I am obliged to perform . . .
operations of great delicacy
on my self."
Was that Berryman, who killed himself?
My memory is as vague as everything else

I try to open myself up, but
the moment I open up, something else shows up
like a vampire under the sun
The words in my soul seem so unlike words exposed to air

Have you ever felt it —

perfect satisfaction when rendered speechless?
I would simply stay speechless if I were allowed
If not, it would be fine just being dumbfounded
wearing something like a pretty ring on my finger
in a total stupor

At the Tidal Flat

The tidal flat stretches out endlessly
I do not see the ocean beyond
I came up with these two lines, but
after that the poem became a mere refrain
As I saw there's nothing pliable
my words could untangle
I sawed off a piece of wood
put some screws into the board and hung a shelf
This is the fact
Metaphors are no use anymore
because the world is so disparate
I remember how scared I felt
when I read a story of Medusa when I was a kid
Now that she turned into stone long ago
I have nothing to fear
How about that?   Metaphors work just like that

I hear water birds call
Is it a song?
or a signal?
or information?
Actually it's none of the above, but a resonance
It spreads into the sky and vanishes in a moment
It is the fact
It is the fact that happens only once, never twice
That is all I find beautiful now

Death and Flame 1940

No one will take my place to die for me
so I will have to die myself
I will become my own bones
not anyone else's
sorrows
streams
people's chatter
spider webs beaded with morning dew
not a single one of these
can I take along with me
may I hope at least
my favorite songs
reach the ears
of my bones?

(Translated by W.S. Merwin with Takako Lento)

Definitions
定義
(1975)

A Very Difficult Object

Its surface is colored gray and white, and its mass is clearly less than half a cubic meter. On one side are letters: Soft White Scotti® Free Fold. It contains precisely 400 sheets of soft white paper, and the utility of the paper is left up to the purchaser. Now, I pull out the first sheet and blow my nose. It occupies a certain space. Therefore it naturally follows the mode of existence in time. I cannot definitively state whether it is beautiful or ugly. Have I already told the readers what it is?

An Impossible Approach to a Glass

It often takes a cylindrical shape with a base, but not a top. It is a depression that stands erect. It is a defined space closed to face a center of gravity. It can hold a certain pre-defined amount of liquid without letting the liquid disperse within the earth's gravitation. When only the air fills it we say it is empty, but even then its outline is shown clearly by light, and the existence of its mass can be confirmed by a level-headed glance, without relying on instruments.

When tapped by fingers, it vibrates to generate sound. At times the sound is used as a signal; at rare occasions, as a unit in music. But the resonance has a sort of stubborn self-satisfaction beyond utility and assaults our ears. It is placed on a dining table. Also it is grabbed by a person's hand. It often slips out of a person's hand. In fact it hides a possibility of becoming a weapon, as it can easily be intentionally broken into pieces.

But after it is broken into pieces, it does not cease to exist. Even if, at that moment, all of its kind on earth were broken to smithereens, we could not escape from it. Even though it is named in a different orthography in each specific cultural confine, it already exists as a fixed idea shared among all. So, even if we are forbidden, accompanied with extreme forms of punishment, to actually make it (with glass, wood, iron, or clay), we would not be free from the nightmare that it does exist.

It is a tool used mainly to quench thirst. But in spite of the fact that, under some extreme circumstances, it functions no better than two palms put together to create a depression, it undoubtedly exists silently as a thing of beauty, in the context of current diversified human lives, at times under the morning sunlight, at times under artificial lighting.

Our intelligence, our experience, and our technology gave birth to it on this earth and named it. We point to it by a string of sounds as if that were a matter of course. Yet, as to what it really is, people may not necessarily have accurate knowledge.

A Personal View of Gray

However white a white may be, it never is a true white. In a white without a single bit of cloudiness, invisibly minuscule black is lurking, and that is always its constitution itself. A white does not regard a black with hostility, but rather it is understood to contain a black because a white by its nature fosters black. At the very moment of coming into existence, a white is already beginning to move toward a black.

But in its long process toward a black, however many gradations of gray it passes through, a white does not cease to be white until the very moment it is totally black. Even when it is infiltrated by what are not thought to be attributes of white such as, for example, shadows, dullness, or absorption of light, a white is gleaming behind a mask of gray. A white dies in a flash. In that instant a white disperses leaving no traces, and a total black rises up. But —

However black a black may be, it never is a true black. In a black without a single speck of gleam, an invisibly minuscule white is lurking like a genome, and that is black's constitution itself. At the very moment of coming into existence, a black is already beginning to move toward a white. . . .

Observation of a Play in Water

To start, her footprints wet with water vanished, and next her cute dimples and innocent eyes vanished. Her pink nails, black curly hair, and knees were gone; by the time the blue sky vanished in a flash, flowers were gone and every possible letter vanished. Of course soldiers vanished as well as tools like gimlets, hammers, pliers and such, which was enough for me to surmise that thoughts must have vanished also. That is to say, all vanished, ranging from the most tangible to the most intangible.

To say "All vanished" to express this condition would be a trite means deployed by indolent poets, but in fact, "All vanished" also had vanished. This means "All vanished also had vanished" had vanished. But allowing no time for indulging in such word games, next moment, a very lively trout appeared, so did, in no time, a stream, a leather briefcase whose owner is unknown, the statute books, and thirteen minutes after two in the afternoon, while lovers were also beginning to appear. Thus in a flash of time, her footprints wet with water appeared again, and the bare tummy and the curled tummy button and the happy broad smile of Miss S (five years and five months of age) also appeared.

CR

Fragments of a Forged Talamaikan Manuscript

タラマイカ偽書残けつ

(1978)

Fragments of a Forged Talamaikan Manuscript

{ [("I don't know exactly where the words I am going to speak now came from," said the old sailor. "It's already been half a century. I happened to be aboard a decrepit freighter, bound for Bombay from Naples. I saw these words, written in Swedish, on some old paper that was being used to wrap a spare teapot. It was hard to say whether they were an epic poem or just some maxims. Attached to them was a simple note: collected from the Talamaika tribe, North Gijin. I memorized them before I realized it, perhaps because I felt so comfortable coming upon my mother tongue after such a long interval. By the time I finished the voyage and arrived at Bombay, I had lost those sheets of paper, but their words were etched into my memory, and today, fifty years later, they are still vivid. I feel as much at home with these words as if they were originally my own." With this the old sailor recited the lines of words recorded below in his hoarse indistinct voice.) So went the preface attached to a fragment of oral literature which one might call the book of Genesis of a minority people called the Talamaika. I first came upon this document while I was in my back yard, throwing into the fire a massive amount of the letters my late father had left. Its yellowed old envelope must have caught my eye because it bore no addressee or sender. On several sheets of paper, probably torn out of a notebook, the words were inscribed in neat handwriting. Driven by my own curiosity, as well as by my greedy hope that I might someday be able to sell this manuscript at a good price as a valuable academic document, I have been keeping this for a long time, but today] At that point the writing, which appeared as a post script, broke off,} he said. When I asked, {What about the main text?} he answered, {What looked like fragments were preserved. I rearranged them in my own way, and translated them into English.} What you see below is my unskilled Japanese translation of the text he recited, with somewhat exaggerated gestures and elocution— the English version of what purports to be an Urdu translation of a Swedish translation from the language used by the Talamaika. So probably it is considerably different from the original Talamaikan[?] text. Besides, I find it difficult to give sufficient credibility to his account of how these lines, probably rhymed originally, survived. As for the region named North Gijin, or the people originally called the Talamaikan, my research showed no trace of their existence. If I am to believe him, the original text in Talamaikan was turned into the second version in Swedish (note: by oral transmission), from which the third version in Urdu was created, which was turned into the fourth version in English, from which follows this Japanese text, the fifth version. But there is no proof that other languages were not involved in the course of the oral or written transmissions. Not only that, it is equally possible that this was originally created in Swedish, or Urdu or English. The man I am referring to as "he" is an American national I happened to become acquainted with, and I have no idea what he does. According to him, he picked up the fragments written in Urdu on a roll of paper at a construction site in a mid-sized town on the West Coast of the United States. He says he found it under a Caterpillar tractor at a construction site where a library was being demolished as part of a new city planning project. But as to the whereabouts of the document, he was vague, saying it was stolen along with his belongings while hitch-hiking. Whatever the truth is, these words surely issued forth from human souls, even though the time, place, and people involved are not known. In order to preempt the unlikely event of any misunderstanding from academia, I name this "a forged document," which, needless to say, by no means negates the words that follow.

I (*there and here*)

My[1]
eyes
went
far.

My
mouth
opens
here.

My
ears
went
far.

My
mouth
speaks
here.

My
nose
went
far.

My
mouth
becomes silent
here.

My heart goes to and fro
my heart goes to and fro.

II (*borders*)

oh
oh
the sun's
beams
glaring brighter than the sun.

At the time
the eyes did not exist
anywhere
I did not exist —
that
I see.

oh
oh
thunder's
roar
resounding fiercer than thunder.

At the time
the ears did not exist
anywhere
I did not exist —
that
I hear.

oh
oh
sulfur's
smell
sharper than sulfur.

At the time
the nose did not exist
anywhere
I did not exist —
that
I smell.

oh
oh
out of its own
out of its own
agirahanamijakuramunji[3]
came to be.

Not by the will
of anybody.
If one looks up at the top
no top
exists.

If one peers down at the bottom
no bottom
exists.

But
there they are.

III (*a hole is pierced for awakening*)

Light's
blade
slashed.
Eyes are slash wounds.

Sound's
awl
was screwed in.

Ears are puncture wounds.

Smell's
skewer
pierced.

A nose is keloid[4]

What awakens
a heart is
pain.

Thus
a mouth is
a pomegranate
split
from within.

IV (*exclaiming is different from making a sound*)

Rain
does not exclaim
rain
simply makes a sound
on stones.

hapituum tem cha.

Bugs
do not exclaim

bugs
simply rub their limbs
in the grasses.

miriru gijiji kukyu chi.

Rocks
do not exclaim
rocks
simply squeak
under their weight.

ooma nooya kooozaga.

Trees
do not exclaim
trees
simply rustle
in the wind.

ssza zazaji fifiluu

Exclaiming are
those that make nests
those that incubate eggs
those that nurse offspring.

Heaving whales[5] exclaim
crystal dragons exclaim
surprised deer exclaim
snow doves exclaim
mushroom mice exclaim

inverted monkeys exclaim
pointed persons[6] exclaim.
cupped persons exclaim.

V (*name*)

Keep in mind
the name of the one
who brought about the first name.

The name is
Kiunji.[7]

Having no shape
it lurks
in the sun
in fruits
in shellfish
in pebbles
in things
completed in a circle
like your head.

Stop asking
what delivered
Kiunji
the name Kiunji.

The one who named
Kiunji
is also called
by the name of Kiunji.

The one[8] who steps out
of a kiunji
will call fingers
ferns
will call smoke
a lizard
will call eagle feathers
lipsa[9]
and will see fire
inside water.

He[10] (who is, though he is not)
steals a look at the center of tantalizing
by his flirtatious glance
draws inconsolable circles
with his shuffling feet
torments his own forged self
with his bare fists.

VI (*what fingers count*)

1[11] splits into 2
2 splits into 3
3 splits into 4
4 splits into 5
Ask the middle finger why.

5 gathers to be 4
4 gathers to be 3
3 gathers to be 2
2 gathers to be 1
Ask the fist why.

Rain Fountain Dews Ponds
Water is connected everywhere
therefore count water as 1.

Fish produce more fish
fish do not change their figures
therefore count fish as 1.

Never forget
1 is the only number that exists
numbers two and more are
all illusions.

VII (*apparitions of great dark figures*[12])

Round and round turning around and around
at the core of the whirl is
nothing
but the force.

Round and round turning around and around
spun out
from the navel
is black thread.

Round and round turning around and around
wrenched out
from the mouth is
black breath.

Round and round turning around and around
bodies dissolve
grass dissolves
bodies and grass mix together.

Round and round turning around and around
an opening appears
becomes a hole
seen through the hole: them.

VIII (*dirge*)

Ah-ha
leafy greens and stone blade[13]
Ah-ha
rosary beads
Ah-ha
that one[14] is gone
grab
what he left behind.

He will turn cold
he will turn stiff
red hair grows[15]
in his eyeballs
green hair grows
on his nipples
He no longer
answers
Now is the time
to stab him with a tongue.

He is going to bloat
He is going to stink
teeth
return to pebbles
hair
returns to thread-like worms
he no longer hits back

Now is the time to
beat him with switches.

Ah-ha
a bow and a string
Ah-ha
karingi[16]
He is gone
Grab
what he left behind.

IX (*songs of those who cannot leave*)

I have come
into a tree
as one who dreams of a tree
   Beat the stones
   Beat with the stones
I retrace
my own birth.

I have come
into a person
as one who dreams of a person
   Rub the bones
   Rub with the bones
I will pass by
my own death.

I have come
into this receptacle[17]
as one who dreams of this receptacle
   Blow the mouth[18]
   Blow with the mouth

I pass down
my own song.

What is already in existence
does not exist
What is yet to come into existence
exists

X (*sayings about the man and the woman*[19])

Going under
beams of snakes
going around
pillars of centipedes
under
a ceiling of leeches
stepping on
a floor of maggots
a woman, however beautiful she may be,
owns
a single
spider.
Holding
a thorny hand
whispering
into mushroom ears
entangling with
legs like ivy
sucking
mossy mouths
a man, however wise he may be,
owns
a corrupt
root.

XI (*Wisdom springing out of nothing*)

When you look back among trees
even though your friends
did not call to you
you
see
yourself
being there
not even being toyed with.

You may
lie on your stomach on the grass
caressing the tips of fern leaves
to devour their roughness
without relying on words

You may
sit on a rock in water
together with fish
to devour its slipperiness
without relying on words.

Between a person and a person
let there be shapes for all
let there be atonement for all
yet
between a person and the sky
only[20]

1 My — This first person singular pronoun does not simply relate to "I" as a single individual. We may consider it a collective first person singular pronoun to represent a number of people who were involved in this narrative, namely this writing, in other words, what you might call bards among the Talamaika, the recorder and translator into Swedish, the old sailor as an intermediary, the recorder in Urdu, the English translator, myself and others. It refers to an entity consisting of multiple layers of "I,"[2] each layer of which is surrounded by a subtle haziness, so it is different from a homogeneous "we," too. Also, the original Talamaikan narrator, whom we might call "archetypal I," carried out the conversion of a so-called state of trance into consciousness. One wonders if that conversion to consciousness also occurred in a trance. There is no evidence to prove that one way or the other, but it is interesting to note that this oral literature opens with the narrator's self-verification.

2 Multiple layers of "I" — When I explained the concept of "multi-layered 'I'" to the English translator, he told me that such a concept is a fallacy. So far as language by its nature cannot accurately define a single "I," every language is merely a pathway from something personal to something apersonal; but simultaneously language functions to prevent a complete depersonalization from happening. Such was the gist of his opinion.

3 *agirahanamijakuramunji* — Noted by the English translator. The word has been transliterated throughout probably because this Talamaikan word cannot be translated to any other language. Judging from the context, one can presume that the word means "one whole entity that cannot be named or objectified."

4 The nose is a scar — In Talamaikan, words meaning eyes, ears, and nose all connote "scars," as I understand it. In order to convey the connotation, the translation reads "the nose is a scar," but in Talamaikan, the same meaning is repeated. The same is true with the eyes and ears.

5 Surging whales — Noted in Urdu. It is not known which of the animals we know now corresponds to the beings listed here.

6 Pointed person — Since it seems almost certain that "pointed person" points to a man, and "a cupped person" points to a woman, for expediency these will be translated as man and woman hereafter.

7 kiunji — The English translator claims that the Urdu version noted that it means "the power to distinguish a certain thing from another," but its basis is not clear. For now, I have recorded the closest phonetic transcription of his pronunciation, but it could also be heard as kyunze (accent on the last syllable).

8 The one who stepped out of a kiunji — It seems to point to a mental patient.

9 lipsa — unknown.

10 He — refers to "one who stepped out of kiunji." The Swedish sailor allegedly explained that this is a special third-person pronoun with no specific gender, which contains the two concepts of the sick and the saint in the Talamaikan language.

11 1 — It would be apparent from the context that the numerals here have subtle differences in meanings from those we currently use.

12 Apparitions of great dark figures — This was probably recited accompanied by some bodily movement, along with the partaking of some sort of hallucinogen. In terms of phonetic patterns, there seems to be a design different from other fragments. What are "apparitions of great dark figures"? They do not seem iconographic. I imagine something like "ectoplasm," for example.

13 leafy greens and stone blade — Presumably the goods the dead left behind were included extemporaneously.

14 that one — Since the English translator orally explained this pronoun as a somewhat insulting third person, with no gender, I used "that one."

15 Red hair grows — As with the two lines that follow, it is not known whether this refers to mold that grows on corpses, or to the ritualistic decoration of the dead.

16 kalingi — unknown. It might be a word to indicate a part of the body of the spouse to the dead, but this is merely an intuitive guess.

17 this receptacle — The Talamaikan language is said to use the same word to signify one's own physical being, a woman's uterus, and the universe.

18 blow the mouth — "Stones" in the first stanza, "bones" in the second stanza seemed to be used as musical instruments. In the same way, one can also surmise that "mouth" refers to an action where two people, facing each other, are blowing their breaths into each other's oral cavity. At the same time, it might signify the mouth to mouth transmission of oral literature.

19 sayings about the man and the woman — According to the Swedish sailor, it is highly likely that this section was supplied later, but there is not much evidence for surmising when that might have been done.

20 between a person and the sky / only — This abrupt interruption, needless to say, is not intentional.

ଊଈ

Selected Poems of
Tanikawa Shuntarō II
『谷川俊太郎詩集　続』
(1979)

To Go Home

When I was born
Earth shed tears to equal my birth weight
I was made from a bit of Heaven and Earth
There was no need to blow the breath of life into me
because both Heaven and Earth were breathing

When I was born
The chestnut tree in our yard gave me a quick glance
I stopped crying for a moment
It was not that an angel shook the tree
it was because the tree and I were brothers

When I was born
the Cosmos gave a smile amid its busy routine
That moment I learned happiness
It was not because I was loved by people
It was just that I came to know how glorious it is to be alive in the
    Cosmos

By and by Death will fold me into its time-honored orderliness
That is to go home. . . .

*("Poems Written When the Poet was 21
or 22 Years Old")*

ଓଃ

Coca Cola Lesson
コカコーラ・レッスン
(1980)

Coca Cola Lesson

That morning the boy came to know words. Of course all his life he had spoken words like everyone else, and was even able to write some. For a boy of his age, his vocabulary was relatively large. In fact he was quite clever at using them to threaten, to cheat, to cajole and sometimes to tell the truth, but that was the extent of it. But now, using words just for such utilitarian purposes seemed to him somehow insignificant.

Something trivial triggered it. That morning he was sitting at the tip of a jetty, dangling his feet just as anyone else would do. During this time tepid splashes from waves wetted his bare ankles. There was no one around he could talk to and it was too insignificant an incident to talk about. But whatever caused it, at that instant, he visualized in his mind the word "Sea" and the word "Me" at the very same time.

Presently he had nothing really to think or speak about. So he mindlessly let the two words "Sea" and "Me" knock against each other like tiddlywinks inside his head. Then something odd happened. The word "Sea" grew bigger and bigger in his head, and brimmed over to merge into the sea in front of him the way two drops of water would, and suddenly they dissolved into one.

At the same time, the word "Me" grew smaller and smaller like the tip of a thin needle, but never disappeared. Rather, the smaller it grew, the brighter it gleamed, moving from his head down toward his center, now floating like a single speck of plankton in the "Sea" that converged with the sea.

For the boy this was an unimaginable experience, but at least at the beginning he was not surprised or uneasy. Instead, he even said, "I see," looking smug. But of course he was not exactly unruffled. He felt a certain powerful force, not his own, well up inside himself.

Rising up before he knew it, he mumbled, "I see, the sea means the sea." Having said that he suddenly felt like laughing out loud. "Sure, this is the sea. It is not something named the sea, but it is the sea." If his buddies were with him, such a monologue would be laughed away. He thought about that in a corner of his mind, and he mumbled again. "I am me. I am, right here." Then this time he felt like crying.

All of a sudden he felt terrified. He wanted to dump everything out of his head. He wanted to make both the "Sea" and the "Me" vanish. He was afraid that his head might explode if even a single word came to his mind. Every single word might turn into something of unknown size and mass, and once any word occupied his head, it might connect to every word all over the world, and at the end he might be gobbled up by the world and die. That's how he felt.

But, just like any boy of his age, he could not lose sight of his own self. Before he realized it, he was trying to pop open a canned Coca Cola which he had bought on his way to the jetty and was holding in his hand. To his surprise he could not do it. Why? Because the moment he looked at the can in his hand, an uncountable number of words like a swarm of locusts swooped down en masse inside his head.

However that was not necessarily as terrifying a situation as he had imagined. Don't run away, stand firm! He opted for the only path to overcome fear, just as he would when fighting against much taller and older boys. In his hand, the can, painted in red and white, radiated words, absorbed words, and breathed as if it were a living thing. Not knowing whether he was tormented or pleased, he faced the swarm of words. But once he separated them one by one, the huge swarm, which seemed like a swirling evil fog, was not at all different from the words on the page of a familiar comic book.

This battle of sorts actually took place in a flash, like in a nightmare. If, for instance, he saw the infinite universe that started or ended at the tip of his can, he was totally unaware of it. One might be able to opine that he named every bit of the unknown about to swallow him with all the vocabulary he could muster, which included his future vocabulary that was yet dormant in his subconscious.

When the totality of words, which can be likened to a single yet-unknown extraterrestrial life, converged into a vision of a volume of the dictionary, the battle was over. The sea was back to being the entity named the sea, and was again calmly undulating. And the boy pulled the tab of his Coca Cola can, and drank up the foaming dark liquid in one gulp, and choked and coughed. "It's just a Coca Cola can," he thought. A moment ago it was a monster.

He stomped on the emptied can, instead of throwing it away into the sea as he always did. His bare feet hurt a little but he stomped on it again and again until the can was totally flattened. He himself was rather embarrassed with the strange experience. He did not even think of telling others about it, nor learned anything from it. Even if he should recall this incident in an incoherent context as he lies in his death bed decades from now, it will have turned into something hard to capture like a whiff of wind, along with all other memories, hence it will surely stimulate his sense different from his declining five senses to frighten him again.

That morning, though, the boy looked down at the flattened Coca Cola can, and simply mumbled, "not for incineration."

Diary on Auntie

I see Auntie crouching on the river bank. Behind her is a large chimney letting out smoke. I can't tell Auntie to do this or do that. Auntie takes a stand. She says she is going to cook devil-root cake tonight.

*

Auntie forgets what she just said and repeats the same story. One moment she is angry, but next moment she is very happy. She cooked such delicious rice before, but now she burns it black. But she doesn't care, because she quickly forgets that she burnt it. Oh what a waste, so burnt up, she says, nonchalantly blaming it on someone else. Inside Auntie, so protean now, the conscientious Auntie of the past is playing hide and seek. Has Auntie gone somewhere else? No, Auntie is here, still. She is alive, with her pretty silvery hair shining in the sun.

*

Oh, you shouldn't, she said, Auntie tells me. A bent nail caught and tore her apron, she says to me. Then the guy just pulled his arms away. A dumb fellow, Auntie says, and she is angry with him. It was some thirty years ago, but Auntie, her nostrils flaring, is seriously angry for some time.

*

Of course what I see is not all of Auntie. Auntie invades me like a virus. Invisible Auntie is more dangerous than Auntie I see, because I begin to lose distinction between her and me. In an effort to see the invisible Auntie I try to describe her. Immunity?
A word like that is of no use.

*

Auntie treasures an earthenware teapot with a chipped spout. When she pours casual tea from the teapot into a teacup, she is most dignified. Then she deliberately begins to follow newspaper pages with her eyes. Captions for a deserted child and for a coup d'Etat are printed in the same font size, so Auntie well understands that there is no difference in importance between those incidents. She has lost three pairs of reading glasses, and she is now using her fourth.

*

There is nothing in this world that can be named clearly. Just as a cooking pot is an assemblage of parts that are not pots, a sorrow is the ruinous end of countless fearsome burdens which are not sorrows. A single name, like a black hole, is apt to suck in all other names. Names take root in anonymity. (For the moment I just leave it this way.)

*

We are going to have a better world, Auntie says. But she says, the world is at best something of this sort. I have seen Auntie crying facing the wall in the evening. All I can do is to keep an eye on her, nothing else. I am so terribly powerless. Because of that, from time to time, Auntie looks to me so incomparably beautiful.

*

I've come to realize the terrifying fact that there is only poetry in this world. Every bit of matter in this world is poetry. That has been the unchangeable fact from the moment words, as we call them, were born. How desperately people have tried to escape from poetry. But that has been an impossible thing to do. How cruel.

*

When she gets hungry, Auntie grabs what's in the pot in her hand and pops it into her mouth. She might take a bath for three consecutive days, then she might not take a bath for a month. She starts fussing saying someone stole a tattered removable collar. Yet, she completely forgets about the stock certificates she hid under her bedding. Auntie is falling to pieces. But inside her is another Auntie. She is like the nesting wooden mosaic box she bought me when I was a kid. I found a box inside the box, and I found another as I opened it, and yet another smaller box inside that. . . . Auntie exposes what she has been hiding one after another, but unlike a box, she never becomes empty. It is silly to ask which the real Auntie is. Contradictions and confusions are Auntie herself. But I sometimes find such an excessively honest Auntie terribly hateful. Because it's me that she exposes.

*

I'm ready for them to come for me anytime, Auntie says. But I cannot die until they come for me, she says. She cannot take care of herself, so she wants to take care of others all the more. You can just leave me alone, she says. I cannot bring myself to tell her that she has no use for pride of that sort. Because I am barely managing to be me just by being in front of her.

*

This world is a square of crazy quilt. Motley colors and cloths are connected in an illogical way, yet the four edges are cut beautifully straight. On the Northern American continent one hundred years ago there must have been aunties very much like Auntie, by a big river, in the shadows of a beech tree, and on the porch of a shack on the fringes of a city.

*

Someday I will become Auntie. I wonder if I am already. My name, my money, my future, or something else of me, none of those can keep me from being Auntie. My hands, my hair, my words, my wandering mind, all I can call my own are so much like Auntie's.

*

Stroking its belly, Auntie is whispering to the dog. Auntie is really happy to see the dog pleased. I cannot keep my eyes off her, wondering if Auntie will keep stroking the dog forever. But soon she slowly stands up, and goes inside. I am left with a feeling that almost chokes me. I simply cannot name it.

⚬

The Map of Days
日々の地図
(1982)

Perspective

"Why am I here?"
you asked me
in a department store on your winter recess
We were riding the escalator
leading to the toy department
You said it as if
you'd just remembered something you had misplaced
giggles, whispers
loud screeches
sugary music
"Why?
You know we are here to buy you a toy —
the soccer game you've been so anxious to get"
"I know that,
but why am I here?"
you asked again
Your eyes looked
straight at me
looking through me
at a distance
no one could see

I wonder if you've learned
from your long-haired young art teacher
about the time when Western painters

discovered perspective
What is close looks large
What is far seems small
What is farther away looks even smaller
Farther beyond that is a single point
where all things disappear
Thus painters learned to depict
what they see in the way they see
But at the same time they also learned
there is a distance humans could never see
However close you get,
there's an expanse you cannot reach
They came to know
the expanse itself is the largeness of the cosmos
You've come from such a distant place
and you are heading toward a distant place
Who on earth could measure
that long road you travel
The single spot
where all disappear
It might be right here
A great big yawn and a sneeze
sniveling and nasal voices
the toy department is full of people
Human lives are swirling here
why are you here?
why am I here? —

"Say, what's wrong?
Are you lost?
Soccer games are over there."
You forget what you asked me a second ago
and pull my arm
Ahead of you I see

the limitless horizon spread
and unknown days
dawning beyond

The City

I unlock the door,
push open the translucent door
walk into a dim room
curve along the wall, hearing my own footsteps
to meet a particular person
I gaze at her glowing skin
unable to do anything

These movements
whisper to each other and stream by me
Their velocity makes up a day
All things around me are bright on the surface
Each has a shape
but will not show what is hiding behind it
Neither does this blue sky in June

Smile

The one I was waiting for appeared
All of a sudden you are walking from between columns
toward me, among unfamiliar faces
in your light warm quilt
smiling

More than any unhappy expressions
smiles hide fearsome secrets

Yet your smile seems so gentle
perhaps because you think
you'd rather be silent than tell lies
You arrived, the one I was waiting for
38 minutes late
you, no one else but you

Unknown Hometown

In this town also there must live a woman
who might love me someday
In this town also there must be good *sake*
and quiet loneliness
that descends on us after sharing *sake* with each other

Leaning against the window frozen white
I am quietly holding my breath
Train, carry me away swiftly

I know I need to go much farther, but
an unknown hometown casts a spell on me!

Path

It is a convoluted path
like yarn too tangled to be undone
while even a maze has an egress
Only the blue sky above is so open

I have been following you
trying to peer over your back
at the distant place you are gazing at

turning at the city street corner at dawn, passing the park at
    noon

along the river in the evening, crossing the overpass at night
I have been following the map of days
but just when I thought I'd hit upon a field with mountain views
I lost sight of your back

Your Back

Your bare back is in front of me
blocking my view
Your vertebrae like a chain are buoys in the ocean
The simile is probably
all I can cling to right now

But I live in the country your back is blocking
The people your back is hiding frighten me
The words the TV is chattering, like cold fingers,
grope for my bare heart
even though it no longer holds secrets (all it has is fear)

Somewhere in the illusory city
on an illusory map afloat in the universe
I forcibly enter my illusory address
I am now at the location
having lost time in a thicket

Even so, you tell me that you like me
with your back that hides all
Before words die inside a big sigh and
unbearable dull pain torments me again
there still is a little bit of a lull

Convalescence

I strolled out to the seaside
having entrusted my injured brain to the hospital
The sea was blue and meaningless
The sand was hot and meaningless
The sky was vast and meaningless
What wonderful meaninglessness!
But, only I
could not become meaningless
I, naked, signified the sea,
signified the sand, signified the sky
and signified the meaning
and I was rejected all alone
Under the bright sun at midday
only I was a seed
that will never bear fruit
But then . . .

I saw
my brain which had escaped from the hospital
begin to eat the sea:
swaying its uncountable folds
emitting a formaldehyde smell
The brain in no time devoured the sea
and it ate me, too, along with it
What digestive power!
Feeling my skin
dissolve inside my own brain
I groaned with pleasure in spite of myself
Now finally I am free
Seeping out of my skin, the container that forms a barrier against all
I reconcile with the sea
inside my own brain

Having eaten the sea, having eaten the sand
having eaten me, having eaten the sky
having devoured the world in an instant
my brain is quietly resting well and satisfied
Inside my brain I am meaningless for the first time
The brain digests the meaninglessness of the infinite world and
by and by it will defecate a beautiful poop of meaning

My beloved brain
will heal like a perfectly ripe fruit
issuing forth a smell like renowned aged cheese
trembling like a failed pudding
unable to manage its mass as big as the universe
maybe it is planning to move to another space

☙

Letters
手紙
(1984)

Time

You remember two
curled-up cats
I recall well-trodden
stone stairs

Because that day will never come back
it comes close to eternity, which
pains us
the one day more elusive than a dream

Today, just like that day
clouds are moving to hide the sun
however much I loved you
it was not enough

A Letter

Right after your phone call
I received your letter
You were playful over the phone
but you were quite serious in your letter
The letter ended abruptly:
"I wish I were a deer living on the savanna."
The next day, Friday (31 degrees Celsius),

we met by the fountain in an underground mall
You twirled your white pocket book
I mimicked Chaplin
then the two of us ate a pizza.

We said nothing about a deer
There are things one can only say in letters
There are also questions one does not dare ask
if one wants to live on
in this world where stars mingle with shoe sores

Your Shoulder

Leaning on
your shoulder in your warm sweater
I say nothing
you say nothing

what a beautifully sung
Mozart
trees are shedding leaves outside
when will I die?

all I need is your warmth, I don't need your heart
as the thought comes to me
I turn my head to see
your eyes intently fixed on me

Poets: Yosano Akiko

I once heard your voice
recorded 37 years after your *Disheveled Hair*
You, at 60, gasped for air
each time after reading a 31-syllable poem
Your voice
stored inside a small cassette tape
reached me
not from the flowering field you adored in your youthful days
but from a dimly lit kitchen smelling of fish
like a strolling singer's song
The seven-five syllable cadences released
your life's secrets hidden deep inside your body
You shed an old-fashioned robe for the sake of love
Your naked body, too bright for eyes,
still shone after so many years
But that start did not foretell your life as a woman since then,
giving birth to eleven children, having to struggle for a living
You wrote "For my own sake I want to stand guard over
my own naked self"
because you knew yourself better than anyone else:
however naked you dared yourself to be
your soul refused to be dragged into the daylight after all
that frustration itself was the fountainhead of your poetry

ୡ

Naked
はだか
(1988)

Goodbye

I've got to go now
I have to go right away
I don't know where
but passing under the row of cherry trees
crossing the main street at the signal
I aim at the hill I always look at
I've got to go all by myself
though I don't know why
I'm sorry, Mom
be nice to Dad
I won't be picky and will eat everything
I think I will read a lot more books too
At night I will look at the stars
During the day I will talk with many people
And I am sure I'll find the thing I really love
Once I find it I will treasure it for my life until I die
So I won't be lonely if I am far away
I've got to go now

A Tree

soon I will become a tree
when the tips of my middle fingers feel a tickle
green leaves shoot out from there
on my ring fingers, on my index fingers, too

lots of leaves grow before I know it and
both my arms become supple branches
and my torso, under my shirt,
turns into a rugged trunk
my toes melt into wet dirt and
lukewarm water seeps into my lower tummy
and I no longer go to school
I don't play baseball or go fishing
I am immobile and stand there at night too
when it rains, it makes me feel real good
no one notices that I am there
everyone hurries by me
I will not go anywhere until I die
I will stand rustling in the wind forever

Piano

When I see Satoru play the piano
I want to eat him up
his fingers are fairer and more slender than mine
I'll start with his ring finger, going crunch, crunch
then, Satoru will not have to be beaten up by anybody any more
he won't have to go to his cram school any more
he can just play the piano as much as he wants
inside me
with Satoru I will travel
to many places
we'll pee in the middle of the desert
we'll listen to winds and rain in a lone shack in the storm
I won't be lonely whatever happens
even when I become an old woman
Satoru will be a kid
even after I die, the sound of his piano
will rise from the earth

ଓଃ

To a Woman
女に
(1991)

Before We Were Born

When you were not yet on this earth
I was not here either, but
we, together, sensed the scent
of the air as lightning dashed across the cloudy sky
and we knew
that someday there would be a day when we would meet
on an ordinary street corner in this world

Birth

That time, too, winds crossed over trees
Loan sharks were counting bills, licking fingertips
A walrus roared in a zoo
Back then, too, the world was a mysterious entity
when you, twisting, moved forward toward light
down the dark birth canal, smelling of blood

A Fist

What was it?
What was it that you were clasping tight
inside your tiny tiny fist,
the thing you were determined not to lose?
You throw it at me
straight at me, even now

Blood

When you bled for the first time
in your fight with the starry sky
I learned to sow seeds
in the barren field of time
Thus we launched the first step of our long journey
toward making peace with death

Day after Day

We lived separate tales in separate families
in mornings when raindrops reach ears, in afternoons when
    winds rattle windows
not knowing they would merge into one
I slept the nights when you did not sleep, but
your days I did not share
were trimmed with the glowing clouds I saw in sunsets

To Meet

At the beginning there was a copy of a picture book and a faded
    photo
then one day two large eyes and
a brusque hello
then words you penned in a free and easy hand
I grew to meet you little by little
before I touched your hand
I touched your soul

Lost

If I get lost you hold my hand to lead me
if you get lost I will also throw away my maps
if I behave affected you will laugh it away
if you lose your reading glasses I will let you use mine
and I will close my eyes and let my head rest on your lap

Telephone

When you fall silent time stiffens
mixed in with the sound of your breathing
I hear someone else's laughter in the distance
I am adrift, with a telephone line as my lifeline
If you hang up. . . .
I have no way of getting back to anywhere

Snakes

You swallow my tail
I lunge to bite at your tail
We are two snakes forming a ring, unable to move
not knowing what is locked up inside our ring

Tomb

We climbed the slope drenched with sweat
The smell of grass choked us
There sat the graceless rock
We sat on the rock and looked over the sea

In no time we will make love crowned by the rock
with our bodies of dirt, with our eyes of mud, with our tongues
   of water

We Laugh

We laugh
we laugh with the mercilessness of the aged
we laugh, on our bellies, peeling lychees
we laugh, though frowning from back pain
we laugh at the ordinary. We laugh at the extraordinary
we laugh with our toothless mouths

A Dream

Two golden babies
drop golden poop under the blue sky
we are in the picture you are drawing
holding each other's hand tight
we toddle toward where time becomes powerless

DEATH

I HAVE BECOME FIRE
AS I BURN I LOOK AT YOU HARD
MY BONES, WHITE AND LIGHT,
WILL DISSOLVE ON YOUR TONGUE
LIKE AN OPIATE

Afterlife

Tangled with each other like two endless melodies
we frolic with the vacuous sky
diaries we kept on a whim, the bed where we slept side by side
ruins and barren fields we visited, matching pairs of worn-out shoes
we entertain fond memories of the little things we leave behind
   on earth

CR

Clueless
世間知らず
(1993)

The Death of My Father

My father died at ninety-four years and four months.

He went to the barber the day before.

Late that night in his bed he emptied all he had inside his belly.

At daybreak, summoned by his nurse, I went to him. His face was the Noh mask of an aged man, his false teeth removed, with his lips slightly apart. He was already gone. His face was cold, but his hands and feet were still warm.

Nothing came out of his nose, mouth or anus. His body was so clean that it needed no cleansing.

Having been told that dying in one's home would be treated as an unnatural death, I called an ambulance. On the way to the hospital, and even after we got there, he was given oxygen and heart massages. It all seemed senseless. I told them so and asked them to stop.

We brought the body home.

My son and the son of the woman I was living with were tidying up the room.

Three people came from the Medical Inspector's office. The time of his death on the death certificate was several hours later than the actual time.

People began to gather.

Condolatory telegrams came pouring in.

Baskets of flowers arrived one after another.

My separated wife arrived. I quarreled with my woman upstairs.

It got busier and busier, and I lost track of what was what.

At night a man rushed through the front door, crying as loudly as a child.

"The Master has died! He's dead!" he screamed.

Then the guy (he came from Suwa) left, saying "I wonder if there's still a train running. I'm going home," still crying

"Offerings" arrived from the Emperor and the Empress. The envelope was stamped with Thirty Thousand Yen.

"The First Order of the Sacred Treasure" arrived from the Emperor. It contained three medals. The lapel pin looked like the dried-up slice of a small lemon. My father used to rub the dry skin on his legs with sliced lemon.

What's called the Associate Third Order arrived from the Prime Minister. This had nothing else attached, but several direct mail sales offers for display frames for medals and their history also arrived.

My father was a handsome man, so he would have looked impressive wearing those medals, I thought.

The undertaker told me the best of all funerals is the cannibalistic ritual.

I thought my father would have to be made into soup because he was so skinny.

*

Death with its quiet and swift hands
brushed away his life's every detail in his sleep, but
for us who chat with each other through the night
in that bit of time before the altar flowers wither
there's no end of silly tales

Death is the unknown
the unknown has no details
that is like poetry
both death and poetry tend to sum up life,
but the bereaved find joy not in a summary,
but in ever-intriguing details

*

Eulogy for My Father

October 16, 1989, at Tōkeiji Temple, Kita-Kamakura

The photograph of my father Tetsuzō and mother Takiko placed at the altar is the one my father kept next to him after my mother passed away five years ago. Along with the photograph he kept her ashes with him. As their son, I am not quite sure whether this was out of love for my mother, or simply procrastination. But today, although I know this is unusual, with the permission of the Priest, I have both of their ashes at the altar. My father directed that my mother's funeral be limited to family members, so the rest of you who knew my mother, please kindly say farewell to her along with my father today.

From my vantage point as his son, my father lived his entire life in the way he wanted. While that may have caused him to be somewhat isolated, I believe he happily and luckily lived out his natural life. I thank you for coming together today to send him off.

*

I was washing a metal ashtray in the bathroom in our old house in Suginami before we remodeled it. My father, in his sixties, wearing a *haori* over a black kimono, came in and said to me that he made a washing machine out of bricks in the same shape as the old one, and that it was working well. He washed his hands and was drying them with a towel hanging all the way in the corner. I thought to myself that I needed to move the towel holder closer to the sink. I asked him if he had any problems. He said he was all right. I felt the same way as I felt just a month ago. The scene suddenly switched to a long shot, and I was looking at my aunt's old house from her yard. At that moment I realized that my father was already dead. Sadness filled my heart and I cried. When I woke, I didn't know if I actually cried or not.

The Path to Kurabuchi

The path to Kurabuchi meanders
only a series of low mountain ridges to the north
there must be a stream to the south — I hear water

In a field gradually sloping toward the ridges are occasional small
    paths
flowers bloom here and there among shrubs
The flowers are unremarkable from a distance
but as we come close by to pick them they are delicate and
    beautiful

On our way to Kurabuchi I picked and bundled flowers with my
    woman
I hardly knew the names of those flowers
even though I know the names of various ideas

We brought the flowers to the small house my father built 60
    years ago
we arranged them in a white porcelain vase mended with wire.
It would be good if I could recall this day after I die
after I forget all words

He Is No More

Is he already dead? I can't believe it.
He does not answer me when I speak to him, but
that has happened many times before
He would be deep in thought, although about what I did not
    know
he would be staring at the yard overgrown with weeds
but he was alive then

But his back like a black lump is still vivid in my eyes
I cannot forget his face expressionless like a mask as I glanced at
    him
Compared to that, his face, now dead, seems more alive
Sometimes people are dead even though they are in fact alive
So isn't it possible that someone can be alive even if he is in fact
    dead?
Maybe that is a privilege allowed only to men, not to animals

I remember of course how he was happily laughing
fond memories
of how he was waving his arms at the time
of the wrinkles on his forehead

But this man who did not respond to me even though he was not
    dead
and the yard overgrown with weeds
are not fond memories
I am waiting for him to say something to me even now

ଔ

The Eighteen Year Old
十八歲
(1993)

A Cosmic World

As the day sublimates into night
I see a cosmic world
beyond clouds burning in the sunset

I wish I'd been born
in a time long past
when the earth was thought to be a flat disk
Then I would have been taught that
the red beyond the burning clouds
was flowing fire at the edge of the great earth
I wish I'd had a secret yearning
(plus maybe a bit of fear)
for that fire

Waiting for the night to arrive
I see the cosmic world
beyond the clouds burning in the sunset

Nov 14, 1949

Late in the Afternoon

The slanting sunlight
colors the edges of oak leaves
then seems to melt into the grass

The awning window in the drawing room
is now a small mirror for a cloud
timidly facing the setting sun

It's been fine all day today
the slanting sunlight
slowly stretches the shadows

Jan 9, 1950

Night Classroom

1

The night school is lit by hundred-candlepower bulbs
They are bare, creating shadows

There are now five shadows on the blackboard
Occasionally they hide the numbers written in chalk once

A chill fills the room
driving the glass panes into a deeper blue

We are students at a night school
we try to beat the chill, but —

2

In my day-school classroom I said under my breath
— are you not sad
that this classroom has no blue ocean? —
And today at the fault line between one cloud and another
I saw an even deeper world

Are you not sad
this classroom has no blue sky?

The "night" is defined in our minds by the glass panes
tungsten does soften the edges, but
between the blackboard and the light bulbs
between notebooks and fingers
inescapable shadows sneak in

Once in my day-school classroom
I yearned for moonlight
Even the moon does not console me now

When the cigarette smoke disappears
when the starting bell rings

won't you fall into sadness
that the night classroom has no blue sky?

3

All the students are tardy
The teacher waits all alone
Think of it. The teacher is alone in that classroom
Lit by six hundred candlepower!
Is the act of tardiness this cruel and mean?
In one brightly lit room a lone figure
All the students are tardy
The teacher waits all alone

4

Embrace hope from night to morning
Arouse the excitement of primeval nights
Prepare to sublimate it into the joy of primeval mornings
(Discords are modified)

Take hope for tomorrow from today
Solid darkness has been destroyed
Breaths are no longer freezing
Now look over at the radiant Sun
Take hope for mornings from the night

c 1949?

❦

Listening to Mozart
モーツアルトを聴く人
(1995)

The Pure Land

I cannot escape from being me
I've unabashedly exposed myself to everyone's eyes:
an ordinary combination of two eyes, ears, a nose and a mouth
This may be because I've had something to hide

When I was reunited with a friend who had just died
in a room surrounded with soiled tiles
he'd had his blood and innards removed and
was thrown onto a dissecting table as if he were a ship-wrecked
    canoe
He was not carrying anything, hiding anything any more
What's left to us was just fluorescent light one might confuse
    with daylight

Brightness is scarier than darkness
Against the shimmering sea, any ugly thing looks beautiful
Facing the unlimited we return to a grain of sand
What reaches our ears is the sound of waves, so unlike jeers or
    laughter. . . .

If I end up at the so-called Pure Land
and if Buddha or the angels see right through me
what facial expressions should I show?

I am hiding
what I surely would have lost if my life were eternal

not knowing that I am hiding it
Surrounded by people's glum looks,
covering my ears against clamoring lives fated to die
I am amid motley shadows of trees in early winter

The Ground

When I sink my head in my pillow the ground pulls at me with
    great force
with fearsome force that puts universal gravitation to shame
I become as flat as a flounder at the bottom of the sea
Only my eyes busily move but there isn't much they can see

If I am to be pulled into Hell, that might be something to look
    forward to
but the ground doesn't seem willing to allow me such luxury
all it wants to do is to keep me flattened onto its face
because I'm liable to forget that I was born out of dust

But soon I fall asleep
In my dream I spring up to the sky again and again
feeling jubilant, accompanied by a passage from a certain
    Requiem,
kicking against the asphalt with my Reeboks, flipping around a
    telephone pole

The model plane I made when I was young was named
    TOTTERING ANGEL
It always fluttered up and fell right away vertically down to the
    ground
From those days onward the ground has been teaching me a
    lesson:
nowhere but on the ground I can live or die

Listening to Mozart

Listening to Mozart he is curled up like an infant
his eyes are wandering over the wallpaper peeling away as if it
    were the blue sky
He looks as if his lover, invisible, is whispering into his ear

Melody, becoming a query, vexes him
but he cannot answer its question
because it answers itself right away
moving ahead of him

loving whispers, so unguarded, directed to the whole world
caresses too tender to exist in this world
prophesies too cruel to materialize
yes to veto every possible no

Listening to Mozart he stands up
he pulls himself free from the music embracing Mother
heads down the stairs to the street looking for queries he can
    answer

ଔ

Rather than Snow White
真っ白でいるよりも
(1995)

Metaphorical Sea

It's not that the man sees the sea
The sea is looking at the man
with a gleaming gaze unchanged since prehistory

It's not that the man listens to the sea
The sea is listening to the man
with innumerable shell ears lurking at the water's bottom

The man sets out on a journey, creating a trail in the water
heading for a horizon that will never fade
the plaything of raging storms and dead calms

Some chopsticks and rice bowls, a few pots and pans and
passions that overflow, undulate, spill out and pool up
will bond the man with a woman

Yet what binds the two more deeply, more forcefully
is this wholeness called the sea
tirelessly recurring yet still beautiful

It is not that the man sings of the sea
It is the sea that sings of the man
It is the sea that celebrates the man

Living with Cats

One morning I got up
to find Meenya dead in a corner of the room
I wrapped him in a towel and placed him on a shelf
He was already stiff as the shelf board
My woman, the keeper of the cat, was still asleep

Meenya was always talking to himself
When I called my woman while we were still living separately
I always heard his voice over the phone behind hers
But as he got elderly he became quiet
He readily sat on a person's lap

That was last September
Shortly after that my father died
I sold some land and a condo to prepare for a divorce
My wife's phone calls distressed me as she constantly changed
    her mind
Even then I was writing poetry in response to requests

Kuro is totally black, has a long tail, and cuts a very handsome
    figure
He'll open the door for himself and go out through the bathroom
    window
As I see him from the back, sitting in the bay window, gazing out,
I believe he understands everything
When he feels like it he comes to lick my hand with his small
    coarse tongue

My woman's son found Kuro somewhere and left him here
He (not the cat, but the son) paints
The animals he paints are all dignified
He arrives in his old orange Beetle
and occasionally he cooks a pork dish for me. That is delicious.

Now that my father is dead, I can see his life more clearly
He was really something
He would read newspapers for hours, silently
sitting by my mother who was bedridden with dementia
"I think I loved Takiko," he said after she died

You say, "I think I loved her," not "I loved her," I think to myself
In his youth he read Goethe
while holding a cat inside his shirt, I was told
In the summer of the year he died, also,
he was constantly reading "Faust" in a mountain hut
eating plain broiled fish from the mountain stream

Fune is colored like a cleaning rag according to my woman, and
    he is quite fat
His tail is very short as if it were broken off
He lives almost entirely for his appetite
He chases waste paper all over the room making heavy noises
He doesn't even know that his name is Fune

We buried Meenya among the trees in front of the house where
    my woman lived
In November my wife put her seal on the divorce papers
My wife will remain angry with me for the rest of her life
My son and daughter are considerate toward me, but I'll never
    know how they really feel

A newborn kitten
comes to meet
with my lap
                — Shūson

We've Got a Baby

This New Year's Day is somehow different from other New Years,
    I thought
That's right, we've got a baby this year

The baby yawns
That surprises me
The baby hiccups
I am so totally impressed

This baby is the child of my child
that makes it my grandchild, come to think of it
in other words I am what is called a grandfather
I thought a grandfather was someone much more impressive, but
now I know that is not so

The baby looks away and frowns
this flusters me
Have I slipped up somehow?
It's not just me, the world of big people is full of slip-ups

When the baby laughs once in a while
I feel relieved
All right, just keep an eye on me
I will show you I can grow to be an impressively tottering old man

Dear Baby
what are you going to be?
Are you going to be a bewitching damsel, a virtuous woman,
a dragon lady, or a heavenly maiden?
None of these are fashionable now
But one day you too will be an old woman
That is unbelievably wonderful

If you don't believe me
just keep on living
laughing out loud, sobbing away,
being dazed, totally focused

letting your little breasts grow
rounded and taut
until they slowly shrivel

Morning Light

Morning light passes through
skimming by your soft skin
skirting around oranges on the table
toward that pier I can see from the window
and to the sea far and farther away

My heart dwells in the shade
fearful of the swiftness of light
yet feeling safe because it keeps on moving

Why is it that what repeats stays forever fresh,
morning light, your smiles, also
the Handel I am hearing now . . .
while what comes but once gets old in a flash?

Among the buzz of good mornings and goodbyes people
    exchange
morning light passes through
My heart is still in the shade
trapped in last night's dream

CB

minimal
(2002)

I.

Tatters

before daybreak
Poem
came to me

robed in
tattered
words

I have nothing
to offer him   I just
gratefully receive his gift

a broken seam
allowed me a momentary peek at
his naked self

yet once again
I mend
his tatters

A brief rest at Suzhou

Pine trees throw shadows on the white wall
peach trees bloom in the open air
fresh green tea leaves are sinking to the bottom of a glass

My life has been riding on
scattered pieces of paper
my regret resides elsewhere
What is far is close by
what is near is
distant

The fortune I picked reads "Lucky"
Such a day full of grace
this is

The room

Like spirits
quarter notes
fly about the room

Music
never reveals
her secrets

Words
court her
in vain

Today
passes away
in silence

To resist

Mountains
do not resist
poems and songs
Neither do clouds,
nor water,
nor stars
It's always
human kind
that resists them

out of fear
out of hate
with too many words

Limbs

Today
I have no one to rely on
but I have my hands

my legs, also
my shoulders
even my face
I utter words
I let words rest
in my heart

With our plates emptied
between us
I laugh with this someone

I sit

One afternoon with the sky covered in thin clouds
I sit on a sofa
like a shelled clam
There are things I must tend to
but I do nothing
simply sitting enchanted

Those that are beautiful are beautiful
Even those that are ugly
somehow look beautiful

Simply being here is
wondrous
I become something other than myself

I stand up to
drink a sip of water
water is also wondrous

My shadow

The river flows gently
Trees bow their heads
to send it off

Turning into my own shadow
I walk along a reddish brown wall
to reach town

Wishing to dissolve
things with physical form

into thin air
Wishing to return
things made of words
back to the quiet
I lie in bed in the dark
to wait for
sleep

And then

When it is summer
again
cicadas cry

fireworks are
frozen
in my memory

a distant country is
hazy, but
the Cosmos is right in front of my nose

what divine grace —
a man
can die

leaving behind
just a conjunction:
and then

Just the way it is

A dear deceased friend is
again at a loss
in front of a travel bag

In the futile search for our souls
we stay behind
sitting in front of almond-flavored *tofu* desserts
The rain has stopped
The sky is made lighter by the sun behind thin clouds
Stock quotes flicker in the town

Everything moves on
just the way it is
heading toward memories

A postcard

A yellowed
postcard
is still here

I scrape off
time
that has accumulated

Until transparent
blood
gathers

Death provides
a phantom
skin

II.

Water

what cannot be learned
saturates
my mind that has lost interest in learning
my eyes see shadows of flowers
my nose smells
innards of fish

the torrential mud of
words
rushes into my ears

my tongue is aged
my skin itches
my body wobbles

my mouth
full of water
is still parched

Deep sighs

The morning sun
shows
the veins of leaves

The sky
hides
stars

A crying child
a smiling dementia
sweat, blood and urine
Nature is
so complete
containing all of these

Sighing deep
not over death
but over life

Night

Night —
from somewhere comes
the sound of water boiling

a trace of
poison is
medicine

a person
violates another
unaware

without words
his heart
drifts

toward another
into darkness
toward faint torchlight

Still life

I am back again
to the still life on canvas
as if it were my hometown

And I am stared at
by those noisy eyes
that gather in the street

I have become water in a pitcher
a bunch of grapes
a piece of cloth draped
Even though I awoke from the dream some time ago
I cannot get out of this picture frame
out of this stillness

Exposed to those
voracious
yet indifferent eyes

Window

What is happening is
so simple, and yet
its roots are so tangled

The sun's rays through the window
do not reach
into my heart

This afternoon when
mice scurry about

in the attic
The window is open
tightly overlapped with
my flat LCD screen

I cannot see
your eyes
in it

Song

Someone
is singing
of me
in a tune of clouds
in a harmony of
trees

someday the rhyming
rhythm of my heart
will cease

but the song will go on
celebrating
you

The melody of water
will flow
along the river bottom

The pause of night
will echo
in the ruins

High noon

A snake crawls
over fallen
leaves

beetles
doze off
in hollows of trees

a man
starts to walk
at high noon

blinded
by brightness
his heart is empty

a scar on his forehead
a scab on his cheek
a tattoo on his chest

he bears
what used to be love
on his back

A pebble

Time
blunts
me

daily ripples
have rounded
my angular edges

my bluish dark
skin
reflects the sky

resting
in a trance
on a child's palm

I roll off
to where there is no shame
. . . . to nothingness

Face

My face —
the only one
in the world

my face —
fate revealed

bewildered
by a faint light
in the depths of a mirror

lost in my search for
another
face

I wait for
the last sunrise
in the night of my heart

Amniotic fluid

Silently
people are
far away

An old
waltz
is playing

Dreamy
quiet
is heard

The past of now
the now
of the past

Secretive
whispers of
amniotic fluid

III.

Giggle

"I gave birth to a fish,"
says the woman,
"I freed it in the sea right away."

I giggle
I am downtown
people are sick of other people

What shall we do now?
Shall we go see
our dead friends?

Here I am, not understanding anything
not knowing anything
I open a pocket paperback for now, but

All that comes to
my mind is:
it's a fine day

The bed

The woman is asleep
another one is also perhaps
in pain, having reverted to being a small girl

Deep behind their covered breasts
their pulsing hearts
mark time

Life puts forth scent
between
the lukewarm sheets

The bed,
while dreaming of love,
brews evil

I myself

Breasts were
a divine gift
faint sounds

the Milky Way
ants on grass leaves
were blessed gifts

at the time
at the place
there I was

That is
I
who return to earth

Blood

Man sheds
blood
in battles

Woman's blood
is shed for
new life

A womb is
a cadenza
that does not sing

The last
fortress
of an uncertain love

A day

Crows cry
ahh,
ahh

At the news of a death
in the morning
I feel relieved

A friend is
discreetly
pregnant

I throw away
crumbled
pressed-sugar candies, and
I wonder about
myself
this afternoon

Taste

There is
no authority
anywhere

only
exposed
genitals
erect
concave
at night

There is already a subtle
taste
of deceit

Winter

Bare branches are
the bones
of the world

Peaceful quiet is truth
desolation is
a pleasure

For some reason
forgetting
why

I walk
in the woods
in winter

Dirt

Memories are
deep
evening darkness

To an aging mind
even regret is
a subtle source of light

Seeds
from many flowers
that no longer bloom

I still keep on sowing them
to make the dirt
sing

Flower petals

Bitter
echoes of
music

My recollection gets moist
my memories
dry up
The petals
of lilies are
carefree

Their honey
fills even
the empty sky

As I am doing now

Though I don't need to
I write
as I am doing now

Lead-colored
calmed sea
of my memories

I write
to one person
in place of speaking

wet sand
at a small
boat landing

what is not yet words
weighs undigested
on my mind

a trail
leads to
a headland

Postscript

Some years ago, for a time, I wanted to be away from writing poetry. It was not because I had come to an impasse. But rather, I came to feel it somewhat distasteful to see myself writing poetry with such ease, and looking at reality only through the eyes of poetry. This might be an occupational hazard for those who have continued to write poetry for many years.

Even so, when I was asked to, I did write some. When the late Yukio Tsuji invited me to his gatherings, "*Yohaku-kukai* [Marginal Haiku Gatherings]" I occasionally dropped in for fun. My hope, probably, was to find some pathway that might lead me to genuine reality. Not through modern poetry, but by way of *haiku,* a short traditional form which I had long resisted. But as I was writing *haiku,* I came to realize that the form was absolutely too short for me.

In the meantime I had an opportunity to travel to China. From the leisurely moments of relaxed journey, some unexpected short poems popped up in me. Before I realized it, I might have become attuned to the direct opposite of wordiness, that is, in tune with *haiku* and possibly in tune with a certain type of classic Chinese poetry. After I returned home, I continued to write linked stanzas of three lines, at my leisure, and came to call them "minimal."

I believe what led me to the short form, which had been foreign to me, was my subconscious desire to be silent, and my desire to return to silence to start writing anew. But I am not sure if I myself have changed, along with the poetic form. Keats said that a poet is a chameleon and that the poet's essence is non-self. I will not forget his words until the day I die.

(*minimal*, August 2002)

ࣃ

Poet's Tomb
詩人の墓
(2006)

Poet's Tomb

In a certain place there lived a young man
Who lived by writing poetry
He wrote a poem of celebration when someone got married
He wrote a poem to be carved on a tombstone when someone died

People offered many things to thank him
Some brought a basket full of eggs
Some sewed a shirt for him
Some just cleaned his room because they had nothing else to
    offer

He was happy for whatever was given to him
He thanked everyone just the same
An old woman for the gold ring she gave him
A little girl for the paper doll she made for him all by herself

He had a name but
People called him Poet. They did not use his name
He seemed embarrassed at first but
He got used to it by and by

His fame reached far and orders came in from distant places
Cat lovers asked for poems on cats
Gluttons asked for poems on food
Lovers asked for poems on love

He did not decline any requests however hard they were
He would sit at his rickety old table
Stare into space for a little while
Then somehow come up with a poem

His poems were admired by everybody
Poems that make you cry out loud
Poems that make you laugh until your stomach hurts
Poems that make you think long and hard

People asked him various questions
"How come you can write so well?"
"What should I study if I want to be a poet?"
"Where do you get such beautiful words?"

But he gave no answers.
He couldn't, even if he wanted to.
All he could say was, "I don't know either."
People said he was a nice guy.

One day a young woman came to see him.
She had read his poems and wanted to meet him.
He fell in love with her at first sight
Effortlessly wrote a poem, and dedicated it to her.

When she read the poem she felt an emotion she could not describe.
She could not tell whether she was sad or happy
She felt like scratching out the stars in the night sky
She felt like going back to a time before she was born.

This is not a human feeling, she thought,
If this is not divine, this may be of the devil
He kissed her like a breeze
She was not certain if she was in love with him or his poetry.

From that day on she lived with him
When she made breakfast, he wrote a poem about breakfast
When she picked wild berries, he wrote a poem about wild berries
When she disrobed, he wrote a poem on her beauty

She was proud that he was a poet
She thought writing poetry was far more impressive
Than plowing the land, building machines,
Selling jewels, or being a king

But once in a while she felt lonely
When she broke a treasured plate
He did not get angry, but consoled her
She was glad, but felt something was missing

When she told him about the grandmother she left behind
Tears fell from his eyes
But next day he'd totally forgotten about it
She thought there was something odd about that

Yet she was happy
She wished to be with him for a long long time
As she told him so, he held her tight to his chest
His eyes were looking into space, not at her
He always wrote poetry alone
He had no friends
When he was not writing poetry
He looked utterly bored

He didn't know the names of flowers, not a single one
Yet he wrote many a poem about flowers
He was given many flower seeds for thanks
She grew flowers in the yard

One evening she was sad though she didn't know why
She clung to him and cried out loud
On the spot he wrote a poem praising tears welling up
She tore up the poem and threw it away

He looked sad
Looking at his face, crying even harder, she screamed
"Tell me something that is not a poem —
Anything will do, just say it to me!"

He stayed silent, looking down
"You have nothing to say, do you?
You are just hollow
All things simply pass through you"

"I live only now in this place," he said
"I have no yesterday or tomorrow
I dream of a place void of everything
Because this world is too bountiful and too beautiful"

She hit him with her fists
Many many times with all her might
Then his body grew limpid —
His heart, brain, bowels, all became invisible like air

Through him a town came into her view
She saw children playing hide and seek
She saw lovers in their firm embrace
She saw Mom stirring a cooking pot

A drunken official came into her view
She saw a carpenter sawing a piece of lumber
She saw an old man choking on his coughs
She saw a tombstone that seemed ready to fall apart

She came to and found herself standing all alone
By the tombstone
The blue sky was as vast as she had always seen it
Not a single word was carved on the tombstone

○ℜ

Watashi (I Myself)
私
(2007)

Watashi (I Myself)

Self-Introduction

I am an old man, short and bald
For over half a century
I have spent my life grappling with words:
nouns, verbs, postpositional particles, question marks and the
  like
Now I rather prefer silence

I do not dislike mechanical tools
Though I love trees, too, including shrubs
I am not good at remembering their names
I am somewhat indifferent to dates in the past
I harbor antipathy against so-called authority

I am cross-eyed, astigmatic and presbyopic
My house has no Buddhist altar or Shinto shrine, but
I have a gigantic mail box that connects directly to my room
Sleep is a sort of pleasure for me
If I dream, I do not remember it when I awake

All the above are facts, but
once I put them down in words like this, somehow they do not
  ring true
I have two independent children and four grandchildren, do not
  keep a cat or a dog

In summertime I am in T-shirts most of the time
A price may be paid for the words I write

.

The River

Earth-colored water hesitates, flows
I realize it is a river
The descendant of formless underground dwellers,
the water is heading toward the sea, that much I know
but I don't know when and how it welled up

As the train crosses the river a young woman next to me yawns
There is something welling up, too, from the shadowy depth of
    her mouth
Suddenly I realize my brain is more dull-witted than my flesh

Feeling uneasy that I, the flesh, riding a train,
am made mostly of water
I, the brain, prop myself up with words

Sometime in a distant past, somewhere in a distant place
words were much less voluminous, but
their ties to the nether world were perhaps much stronger

Water remains on this planet
morphing into seas, clouds, rains and ice
Words, too, cling to this planet
morphing into speeches, poems, contracts and treaties

I, too, cling to this planet

To Meet "Me"

Veer off the national highway onto the prefectural road,
turn left again onto a village road and come to the end

"Me" lives there
It's a "Me" that is not myself
It's a modest house
a dog barks at me
some vegetables are planted in the yard
As always I sit on the ledge of the house
a cup of roasted-leaf tea is served
no greetings are offered

I was given birth by my mother
"Me" was birthed by my words
Which is the true me?
I am sick and tired of this topic, but
as "Me" suddenly starts to wail
I choke on my tea

The shriveled breasts of a senile Mom
that's the dead-end of my birthplace,
says "Me," sobbing terribly
But as I gaze at the daytime moon in silence
it slowly begins to settle in my mind
that the beginning and the end go farther than that

The day has ended
Listening to frogs
we fall asleep in futons placed side by side
both "Me" and I are now <the sparkling dust of the universe>

Certain Scenery

The twister is at a loss, not knowing where to go
having risen in a field where not a single creature is around
Profuse tears, vaporized, turn into puffy clouds
to float in a corner of a dying blue sky
Corpses are scattered here and there among grass

no birds are there to pick at them
the remnant of what was once called music
drifts like a timid guardian spirit

All the words people thought, spoke, and wrote for generations
were corrupt from the outset
only a silent smile directed at a new-born puppy
was true
the sea laps away, coming ever closer to the mountains
the stars, one, and then another, close their eyes to expire
Is it because "God" is still around?
or because he is already dead?

The end of the world is as serene and beautiful as this . . .

I write down these words —
The words hold just my past
I don't see the future in them anywhere

It's Morning

First I stretch myself in bed
I rise up in one breath
I go take a pee
I fetch newspapers
I am a minuscule power plant

The power of dry leaves falling
The power of tears from a fussing child
The power of the resonance of a Jews' harp moving away
The power of casually placed punctuation
The power of Good Morning!
An invisible matrix

Unites minuscule powers
I am one of its joints, too
A globe is placed on the table
I try to stare down the Earth

I drink a glass of carrot juice
I turn on my desktop computer
I sit unfocused for a little while
Unexpected words come to me
Like water bubbles, like now

Goodbye

My dear liver, it's time to say Goodbye
It's time to part with my dear kidneys and spleen as well
I am about to die
but no one is beside me
so I will say goodbye to all of you

You've worked for me for quite a while
you are going to be free now
you may go wherever you wish
once I part from you I will also be free
I will be just my soul, naked

My dear heart, I caused you trouble and palpitations
My dear brain, I caused you to think of trivial matters
My dear eyes, ears, mouth and penis, you worked hard for me
Don't, all, think ill of me,
I was what I was thanks to you all

Having said that, my future without you is bright
As I will feel free of myself
I will not hesitate to lose myself

to dissolve into dirt, to disappear into the sky
to become part of those with no words

Continuing to Write

A train runs on a single track along the gorge
monkeys have given up on evolution
familiar bagpipe sounds are receding
and I have no choice but to continue writing poetry

A mother sits on a sofa, nursing her baby
a sudden explosion surprises a midday street corner
opinions are noisily voiced in a new morning
a youth is sulky, reading comics

so what do they matter?
An official history lines up only heroes
projecting old scarred images
and I have no choice but to continue writing poetry

I cannot find the end
because I don't know the beginning
Day after day I live with doubts about believing
Only the sky is limitless, like salvation

I live with refuse that has no place to go to
forgetting the names of missing persons
pawning off offerings to the altar
unable to distinguish nanometers from light years
Asked about pros and cons in rapid succession
I dodge my swaying moods
I seek supreme bliss deeper than meaning
I have no choice but to continue writing poetry

I Am Me, Myself

I know who I am
I am here now
but I may be gone in an instant
even if I am no longer here I am me, myself
but in truth I do not have to be me

I am a plant at least a little
I may be a fish more or less
I am also an ore with a dull sheen
though I don't know its name
and of course I am almost you

Because I cannot disappear after being forgotten
I am a rhythm in a refrain
I am ephemeral undulation and a particulate
having arrived, if I may be so conceited,
riding on your heart's beating rhythm
from the light years of distance

I know who I am
so I know who you are
even if I don't know your name
even if there is no census record
I am crowding out into you

Feeling happy being wet in rain
feeling at home with the starry sky
cackling at crude jokes
I am me
beyond the tautology of "I am me"

Deserted House I

A woman came into the house
From another door a man came in

Silently the man undressed
So did the woman
Her right hand touched his lower belly

The town looks hazy through the drab glass pane
His fingers pinched her nipple
Muffled voice
The man came into the woman

On the filthy floor
two bodies undulated like the sea . . . then calmed down
In the distance guns sounded as if corn were popping

Silently the man dressed
so did the woman

The man left the house
From another door the woman left

Deserted House 2

Remove a floorboard
there should be a diary hidden there
Clusters of words, hoped to be read
while refusing to be seen,
quietly fade on the paper
Their specificity is almost meaningless now, but
their connotations just manage to suggest echoes of a joyful life
"August 6th Fair

<God> does not speak in human language
It speaks in the language of the sky, the wind, and birds,
in the language of rocks, centipedes, and poisonous mushrooms:
a language that humans cannot hear unless they obliterate their
    own —
The first mistake humans made was to name it <God>"

Savage plants break through the floorboards invading the room
A long line of ants marches toward the tilted cupboard
What was once called God
does not cease telling tales

Deserted House 3

Dust covers an upholstered chair
A toy figurine, its arm broken off, is abandoned on the floor
Someone carried off time before it became memory

The wind softly rattles the window panes
Is it my heart, or my mind, or my soul that it threatens?
This place has too many elements difficult to name

Two translucent silhouettes are embracing to kiss
Fragmented stories and national borders
Tides slowly move in from a distant ocean
Countless documents grow quietly submerged unnoticed
An artless beach ball is afloat
Spider webs, invisible, hang across all
Where are they living now
those who once lived here?
They may be us

Before sinking like Atlantis to the ocean's depth
countless strobes emit light
Tomorrow flits by

Falling Asleep

Crows cry in the distance
What do they want, calling so persistently
in the middle of the night like this?
Somewhere a washing machine is groaning
Strange sparking noises come from the ceiling

Dark space prevails outside the house
It should be filled with life
but the word VOID comes to me

[*a dead body's hair grows, its nails grow*]

Since when has the world been assembled like this?
Sounds I hear in my sleepless night
turn into music of the absurd in my heart

*

I rise to arrange words on paper
even though there's nothing I want to say
because I want to let words be like pebbles

Over-abundance of meaning is powerless before violence
so are tears
so is silence of course

[*a fetus's hair grows, its nails grow*]

But the silence, lurking in words,
in the guise of
laughter at times
meaninglessness at times

or a song at times
lures people to the edge of this world. . . .

*

A world that revives through the recollection of a profound
    orgasm
exists like magma
on a dimension different from reality

In that crucible I wait,
in and out of dreams,
making a hodgepodge of
races, religions, systems, thoughts, and fantasies
for the hushed first cry of a newborn

Two by Ten

Over the rubbish of speeches dripping from this planet
poetry, the morning mist, listlessly lingers

The cheek I touched with my fingers that day
is now merely a line on a white sheet of paper

The tongue does not speak but licks
what eyes have failed to see

Each moment that my mind forgets
piles up in my soul (or does it?)

Tired of walking down the narrow road of words
I crouch in the maze of silence, and laugh

A dictionary cannot fathom the depth of a single word
the shoal of intellect is littered with vocabulary

Language is the skin; it sticks to reality's flesh
poetry is an endoscope; it stands paralyzed before nebulous
    viscera

Silence has yet to do its work
after the irredeemable splendor of figures of speech

Meanings call for meanings
unable to bear the forlornness of dusk

Night grows deeper and deeper, at its bottom
tomorrow exudes a subtle scent

Looking at the Yard

I know
you no longer read poetry
dozens of books of poetry you once read
still line the shelves in your bookcase
but you no longer open those pages

Instead you stare through the window pane
at the small yard overgrown with weeds
as if to tell me you can read
invisible poetry hiding there
keeping your eyes on the soil, ants, leaves and flowers

"Sally is gone, no one knows where"
you recite in a voice that is not quite voiced
is it a line you wrote
or a line by someone else who was once your friend?
even that no longer matters

What spilled from words
what brimmed over words
what stubbornly rebuffed words
what words could not even touch
what words murdered

unable to mourn or celebrate any of those
you are looking at the yard

A Poet's Ghost

A poet's ghost lingers
on the other side of the window pane of a deserted house
where raindrops are coursing down
not satisfied with the place he occupies in a corner of literary
    history
not satisfied even after driving a woman to her death
not allowing himself to be settled in the other world

He can no longer raise his voice
but he is there, having turned into voluminous writing
At the deep ends of the bookshelves in the basements of new
    and old libraries
he is still competing with his good friends for fame
unable to answer the queries poetry has posed him

He believed he'd fathomed the heart of the blue sky
He believed he'd learned the reasons for small birds' calls
He believed he lived among people like their pots and pans
and that he deeply understood the silence lurking inside screams
    and whispers
without losing a single drop of sweat or blood

By the poet's ghost stands the ghost of a rhino
questioningly peering at his neighbor
The rhino doesn't know the poet was also a mammal
People, please sing them a lullaby, treat them alike —
the poet and his dead friend

In Defense of Poetry or Why Novels Are Dull

"Poetry is busy doing nothing"

— Billy Collins

It is not I who rudely scatter footprints of MS fonts
all over a notepad screen as white as the morning of the first
    snow
That's what novels do
I'm so glad that I can only write poetry

Novels seem to be full of serious worries
Should a woman carry a no-brand pocketbook or
a Gucci bequeathed by her late mother?
From there unfolds an endless story
of confused tyranny, love and hatred —
Good grief!

As for poetry, at times it floats softly in the sky, unaware of itself
Novels revile such poetry as "heartless" or "too naïve"
That I do sort of understand

Novels trap humans inside a cage of hundreds of pages of words,
    and then
have them dig an escape tunnel
If they succeed in digging the tunnel, where to?

They find themselves at the end of an alleyway in their childhood

There, they'll see poetry standing nonchalantly
along with a persimmon tree and the like
Sorry about that

A novel's job is to describe human karma
Poetry's job is to deliver unbridled joy to humans

Novels walk down meandering paths leading to neighborhoods
Poetry skips down a path stretching straight over the horizon
Neither can fill hungry kids' bellies, but
poetry at least doesn't begrudge life on earth
Because poetry takes to heart the happiness of a breeze
losing words would not scare it

While novels struggle, looking for egress for souls
poetry happily warps in time and space,
singing in a dotty voice that equates the universe with worn
    shoes,
riding on rhythms imparted orally by ancestral spirits
heading toward the day after tomorrow when humans don't have
    to perish   .

Epitaph for "Poet's Tomb"

"I, infinite silence, will grant you words"

[God Contemplates Man]
— Jules Supervielle

When I was born
I was nameless
like a water molecule
But right away I was fed vowels mouth-to-mouth
consonants tickled my ears
I was called and
pulled away from the cosmos

Oscillating the atmosphere
carved onto clay tablets
inscribed on bamboo
recorded on sand
words are onion skins
If I keep on peeling
I will not find the cosmos

I would have loved to lose words
to be a tree singing in the wind
I would have loved to be a cloud from a hundred thousand years
  ago
I would have loved to be a whale's song
Now I go back to being nameless
with dirt over my eyes, my ears and my mouth
with stars leading me by the fingers

Nothing but Words   *dedicated to Chūya**

Having become nothing but words
mountains crouch in a stupor
the harbor is mulling something over
under a sky covered with thin cloud

I wonder if it is the same in other countries
the sea simply separates one land from another
even a sinner's deeply sorrowful interjections
have turned into nothing but words

A shrewd merchant intent on making money
rolls in electrons in a bathtub
Love letters I wrote a long time ago
are now nothing but words

The blue veins bulge on the nape of the neck
of a young woman cruelly tied up
Poetry is about to peel away from the cosmos
having become nothing but words . . .

That's not true! Not true at all!
It's far from being merely words!
Didn't a feudal page stab his thigh with his short sword
in an effort to keep himself from dozing off?

— Silence
all we have left is silence
A scarecrow stands crestfallen
meditating with its straw head

---

*Nakahara Chūya (1907–1937), poet.

Warm white rice is steaming
in matching bowls for a man and wife
on a dinner table somewhere
its warmth is softly rising

Music

With a gracious nod
the *andante* comes to an end
two chords are momentary visitors
having come from a distance that meanings do not reach
they are on their way home

A spider is swinging in the wind
at the end of a thin ephemeral thread
as I am looking at it
the *finale* starts
heralding the silence at the end

With all their thoughts
sucked into the cave of time
people are alive unguarded
as clean as mountain streams now
in love with the cosmos

"The River of Sound"   to Takemitsu Tōru

The river of sound flows between one tree and another
between a cumulonimbus and a corn field, too
perhaps between a man and a woman, too

You make its undercurrent resound in our inner ears
with the piano, the flute, the guitar, and voices
sometimes with silence

Music never becomes a memory however much time passes
because it makes the present echo into the future
you are here forever, too

I put on the clothes you left on this shore and
listen to songs by you on the other shore
Dusk descends slowly over the trees surrounding this hall

Dictates of words slowly recede into the background
we sense around our ears
warm sighs of a universe filled with contradictions

Where Is He?

I saw him in the summer
I heard his voice in the fall
I was able to tap him on the shoulder in the winter
but spring never came around with him

Yet he visits us over and over again
bringing sounds from beyond silence
to our ears

Our eardrums delicately vibrate
coming in touch with waves from the invisible world —
another reality beyond meanings
created with tonal atoms

There he is
attentively turning his healthy ears
to sounds freshly born, to voices ever reviving

Quoting "Quotations from a Dream"

Water dripping
. . . ripples
silently

Sound is
looking for a place
to return to

Shadows
secretively
come closer

Premonitions in the waves
palpitations
in the wind

Beastly whispers of love
minerals'
sweet nothings

A flower
peers into
the abyss

All of a sudden
a clown
and a princess

Time
marks
a comma

A memory is
tickled
into smiling

The castle
the garden and
the dried-up fountain

Fragments
of a bitter
dialogue

Growth rings
answer
as why's arise

Divine silence
lurks among
scattered electrons

Like the tail
of a recurrent
comet

Stirring
of souls
of trees

Where are people?
somehow so
distant now . . .

The horizon
rejoices
sharing eternity as a backdrop
In the vacuous sky
embryos of stars
sing .

Eleven Variations on "Late in the Afternoon"

The slanting sunlight
colors the edges of oak leaves
then seems to melt into the grass

The awning window in the drawing room
is now a small mirror for a cloud
timidly facing the setting sun

It's been fine all day today
the slanting sunlight
slowly stretches the shadows

Jan 9, 1950

*

In the slanting sunlight
children have slowly scattered
to go home
On the bench an old man closes his book
coming out of the shadows of history
The power of reason has cast light
only on sinister lethal weapons
like guillotines to start with
The old man raises himself leaning on

Watashi (I Myself)

an ephemeral memory of love
lurking in shadowy smoke-like twilight
He leaves the park to return to his institutional "home"

*

A tree grows toward the sky
recording itself in its growth rings

A man also stretches himself to the sky
and drifts out into the universe, but

unlike growth rings
his history has no center

In the slanting sunlight
a treetop is a golden arrow pointing at heaven

I want to live like a tree
believing

the center, the moment of birth,
connects straight up to the cosmos

*

"You are a transparent sheet of glass"
says a woman
"You can't hold light inside you
because you are afraid of shadows"

"You are a mirror"
says a man
"You reflect light altogether

you may be afraid of shadows, too"
Trying to mimic slanting sunlight
the lighting engineer is sweating behind the scenes

"Somehow these lines embarrass me"
says the woman
"Is the light meant to be a metaphor for reason?"

"If so the shadow is the subconscious"
says the man
"light cannot reach viscera, either"

"Visible light can't do that"
says the woman
"but invisible light pierces us
with no limit"

*

One afternoon at the deep water's bottom
Sea-God's Palace is in total silence
It's been a long time since Sea-Princess passed away
shellfish emit pale blue light
sea-plants yield to the ocean's motion
time does not tick here
it only sways in a slow swirl
from time to time sonar pings from some country's warship, but
the Palace gate, inlaid with mother-of-pearl, stays shut
waiting for Armageddon

*

A small firearm is placed on a tea-table
a man, bare-chested, is playing the cello next to it

yellowish sunlight is coming through shutters
the story is relaxed at this point, but
soon a police squad will circle this house
the man will be shot to death, rehearsing Bartok
. . . this plot is beginning
to bore the author (a woman 36 years of age)

Yellowish sunlight reaches into her old white Mac
like in the story
a black cat is curled up on the couch

From a distance a chime, a children's song of sunset,
reaches, not the story, not this poem
but my own ears as I write this, here and now

*

In a shop named "Afternoon Tea"
drinking a hot cup of *chai* a thought came to me:
Meanings grow like mold on people's minds
Weren't words less verbal in ancient times?
Weren't they just there, not tormented by meanings,
like a chipped tea cup?

Music, different from murmuring background music
softly sings
in the depths of me

*

The boys are beginning to rise up in the woods
Because their parents and teachers don't answer their morning
    queries
they decipher, without realizing it,

the shadows growing in sunlight filtered through leaves
They can't count on adults
they need to head for the sea

They can't trust folktales or fairy tales
They go out of the woods, down a narrow pebble-strewn path
but they are already lost
a small lizard watches them from the grass
a kite is peering at them from under the cirrus
no one helps a boy as he trips and falls

The sea is calling to them from a distance
but they need to age before they learn what it means
As the downy hair on their cheeks begins to shine gold
the boys gradually slow their pace
finally come to a stop
Where are the girls . . . ?

*

She arrives late in the afternoon and says
"Look, I found it on the beach"
a piece of glass, polished and rounded by waves,
a pale blue piece like a large tiddlywink

"It's so ordinary
but beautiful . . . I feel it's so very beautiful,"
she says, looking as if she is about to cry

She is no longer young
Neither am I. An old friend from our childhood has died
Tonight is the viewing

Nothing special, something no one cares about

something no one knows why it has to be there
"I feel for things like that"
I put on my black tie, listening to her voice

*

I wonder what I am like in your fantasy
the face reflected in the rippling water —
is that really mine?

Words extend uneasy feelers toward words
Projected images flicker only to dissolve into darkness
In your fantasy I count the number of afternoons already gone
My sorrows infiltrated by the golden gleam —
were they also born out of my mother's womb?

There are questions one must not answer with poetry
you told me so one time
Who was I at that time
in your fantasy?

*

"Is all our life, then, but a dream
Seen faintly in the golden gleam
Athwart Time's dark resistless stream?"

— Lewis Carroll

*

There's something I have missed writing down, I think
perhaps something like balls of dust, no
something like nebulae millions of light years away
There's something I missed writing down

in a letter? in my diary? in my poetry?
Something I missed writing down
something I hesitated to put into words
where is it now?
A full-length mirror reflects the grass from 60 years ago
a young man is walking this way
Would I recall it if I spoke to him?
if I walked up to embrace him, if I stared into his eyes
if I reviled him, beat him, stabbed him?
Or is there nothing I have missed writing down anywhere
even if I can recall it?

The Boy

A Cloud as a Signpost   The Boy 1

Scattering spores of light
the boy is waving his arms as hard as he can
He cannot help but keep going
in the direction he has been told not to

How is he choosing his way
among many divergent paths?
With a cloud as a signpost as it gently changes its shape
his gait is light, his eyes searching

Because he does not know his real destiny
he hears mountains, deep woods, and shallow streams like songs
until someday the hurt he'll suffer in heart and body
begins to cause him pain

With beasts, birds, and insects as companions
far away from his mother and his brothers,
unaware that he has long lost his way
the boy already blends in with the scenery

Grass of Life   The Boy 2

Music goes on forever
so I cannot stay here
I cross over the starry horizon
to walk on the grass of life

Mom will pass on someday
Dad, too, walking with a stick
will one day depart from this transient home
leaving me a memento, an empty glass bearing his fingerprints

That's OK, I think
Nothing comes to a definitive end
because each and every thing is beautiful
Wildflowers I picked on my way are already among my fond
   memories

When goodbye becomes hello
I come home from a distant journey
with an invisible souvenir in my arms
accompanying a sister who was never born

My Future Puppy   The Boy 3

A puppy who will love me some day
wags his tail on the terrace of a lone house on the headland
Until I get to meet him
I will keep my diary every day

about a horse chestnut tree in the woods one day
about a charley horse in my leg one day
also about a beautiful orphan another day
as I grow up little by little

Yesterday I visited the planetarium by myself
I saw the starry sky of thirty thousand years ago
It slowly circled above my head
Tears came to my eyes though I didn't know why

The day I will be no more
the stars will shine as always
Maybe my future puppy
will be with me

To Meet Mom   *The Boy 4*

I went into the past all by myself
In the cloudy sky of long ago butterflies flutter
A girl is looking at them
alone, sitting in the grass

When and where was the feeling of loneliness born?
Sitting next to the girl who does not say a word
I watch butterflies mate
This girl might be my mom

A path no one has yet taken
stretches before me, disappearing into the horizon
only a stringed instrument's faint sound
anchors me to this world

When the distant future becomes the past,too
I will surely be here
I will have learned to love
and to feel joy even in dying

Into Music   The Boy 5

And then I walked on inside music
no one was around but
the plaza was brimming with life
embracing the deep ocean beneath

The lifetimes of invisible trees passed by
sins shuddered at a premonition of forgiveness
memories of a prince blended with those of a serf
stars' eggs were crowding the entire sky

My body became transparent
my feelings in the depth of my peach-colored guts
fanned out to the end of the universe
and spilled over its edge

And I've come back
relying on the faint light of my power amp's vacuum tubes
because I know what dwells there
is also the proof of my being alive

I Am a Human   The Boy 6

I am an aged boy
an old man as yet unborn
The all-knowing Sun has been
silently granting us light for billions of years

I am a human
not an iguana, nor a mushroom
sometimes wishing to be a cumulonimbus cloud
sometimes yearning to be a sperm whale
My sister left here last year

leaving a stubby lipstick behind
I don't need to go anywhere
because anywhere in the world is here

Traveling down the veins of a dry leaf
I draw a map of my life
facing the direction my penis sharply points to
my dream will awake

Rainbow Gate   *The Boy 7*

Down the river of words from everyone's chatter
drifts a bamboo-leaf boat carrying a little anguish
I stand still on the riverbank of life
to silently breathe in the scent of water

The mind can travel anywhere
however far it may be
so I am happy that there are things I have yet to learn
even if knowing them brings me more anguish

As a soldier dies in a desert
may an excruciatingly cold spring well up beside him;
from there
may a story yet untold suddenly begin

Was I fond of someone yesterday?
Will I fall in love tomorrow?
A rainbow has appeared like a gate to somewhere
Some day I want to go through that evanescent gate

What Grandmother Says   The Boy 8

"Everything, just too much"
Grandmother says, sitting in the middle of a room
though she has thrown out a lot of things
though she has let go of many things

Grandmother's universe is bulging
with uncountable stars
with babies ceaselessly being born
with human words spoken and written

"Everything, just too much. Just too much"
It is my father's mother who repeats it like a mantra
She cannot feel rich even though she has too much
so she can no longer tell any tales

With her pretty face with thinning eyebrows
mauled by memories she cannot let go
Grandmother builds in me
fragile cairns to future

You Who Are Weeping   The Boy 9

Sitting by you as you weep
I imagine a grassy field in your heart
There, where I have never visited,
you are singing to the vast open sky

I like you weeping
just as much as I like you laughing
sorrows are around everywhere anytime
at some point they surely dissolve into joy

I do not ask you why you are weeping
even if it's because of me
now in a place out of my reach
you are embraced firmly by the world

Inside a drop of your tears
dwell all people of all times
I will face them and say
I like you weeping

My Love   The Boy 10

Just loving her
will complete my life
After I die
I will live on in her memories

The blue sky that spreads wide over her
was once mine only
I will not let anyone else claim
the Sun that casts light on her cheeks

Beyond mountain ridges covered with snow
there is a village where she lives
She will bear her children there and
will be surrounded by her grandchildren

Happiness is as ephemeral as a mirage
It stays underground forever like a fossil
I can already see
her serene gaze

Music Again   The Boy 11

Somewhere, sometime
someone played the piano
The notes, even now, transcending space and time,
vibrate the air and caress my ears

Sweet whispers from a far far distance —
there's no way of deciphering them
all I can do is to give myself up to them
like a tree rustling in the wind

When was the first note born —
a cipher from some presence
in the midst of the vacuous universe
stealthily enigmatic?

No men of genius ever created music
All they did was simply close their ears to meanings
humbly turn their ears
to the silence that has been there from time immemorial

Goodbye Is a Temporary Word   The Boy 12

I part from the evening glow
to meet with the night
But the dark red clouds do not go anywhere
they are simply hiding in the dark

I do not say good evening to the stars
because they are always lurking in the daylight
The *I* at the time of my being a baby
is still at the center of my growth rings

I believe no one vanishes
My late grandfather is a pair of wings growing from my shoulders
They take me to some place that transcends time
along with the seeds left by withered flowers

Goodbye is a temporary word
There is something that ties us together
deeper than memorable events or memories
No need to pursue it, as long as we trust it

Immortality

Immortality

You fly
above the sea of clouds
with no wings
freely, happily
though you are in awe of the sky

You fly
not to flee
not to pursue
uplifted by air
because of love

You fly
commanding a view of invisible houses
along the invisible river
imagining invisible mountain ridges
soaring high

You fly
spurning envious gravity
commanding a bird's-eye view of dynastic changes
looking down at a number of mushroom clouds
toward immortality

With a Rabbit

Let the rabbit be on soft grass,
he thinks,
placing the rabbit
on the soft Spring grass
gently so it will not be afraid

The world is not coming to an end yet
but everything is so uncertain
that at least he wants to hold
the rabbit in his own arms
to climb a hill
on foot
away from the aimless city

There remain
matters not yet written in books
In that open margin
he is with the rabbit

to hear
a song like a fading oracle
blend into the wind

Under a Tree

A child sits
alone
with his knees together
far away from everybody
Time, like a mist, enwraps his shoulders

The moon is shining
Sunbeams are cascading
Stars are orbiting

No one can determine where that is
No one knows the path to get there

A frog is looking up at the child
An elephant leans close to the child

Flowers are still in bud
In the quiet the universe reveals
mysteries hidden at the inmost center of the child

The child sits
smiling softly
for us who are growing old

CR

Tromsø Collage
トロムソコラージュ
(2009)

Ferry to Death

Before I realize it I am on a ferry boat bound for the other world
It's pretty crowded
Many are elderly, but there are some youths
Surprisingly I see babies here and there too.
Most are alone
but there are some couples huddled together looking scared

I have been told that it's not an easy task to get to the other
    world, but
if I get there by just being rocked on this boat, it looks easy,
I think to myself, but the thought is somehow amorphous
I am not sure if I actually thought that
Is this because I'm dead, or
are feelings like that by nature?

I happen to look up. There it is, the sky is here, too.
it is the late afternoon light of the early fall as the sun is
    beginning to set
fleeting orange veils over faded blue
like a dream one keeps on dreaming while trying to wake from it
The ferry moves on, groaning with low, old-fashioned engine
    noise
I wonder if the other world is still far away

An old man next to me mumbles, as if he's talking to himself
"Is this, do you think, the River Styx?

Much larger than I imagined, you know. It looks like the sea."
Now that he mentions it, I cannot see the other shore.
But I cannot see the horizon either, which means
the sky and the water are a continuum like a single sheet of cloth

Wait, I hear a voice from somewhere
It is saying, "Honey, Honey!"
It sounds like crying
The voice sounds familiar; that's my wife's voice
She sounds somehow oddly erotic
I want to hold her, though I don't have a physical body any more

I glance around, looking for my wife
She is right here, but faded like a ghost
I hold her hand, but have no tactile sense
Instead I understand her feelings like my own
She is deeply sad, that's fine, but
she is also taking life insurance into account, which I do mind a
    little

Even my wife's wailing doesn't convince me that I'm dead
This is like an extension of my living days
Come to think of it I've never really felt I was alive in my life
I wonder if I was on my way to death already back then
the fog horn yawns with a silly sound

a flock of birds are circling above the ferry
they are the souls of those yet to become buddhas
I once read a tale about them
If I become a bird
I won't be able to chat with friends and family who died ahead of
    me, will I?
Or maybe our human tongue is useless here?
No need to worry —

one of the birds calls to me from above
I can't hear its call, but its feelings ring in me
It's a girl who was my age and lived next door but died at five
"Mom hasn't come to me yet
Flowers never wilt here, you see"

There are many things I want to ask her
but since she's just like she was when she was a five year old, I'm
    at a loss
where is this ferry heading?
what do you do in daytime?
can you see stars at night?
whatever I ask
all I get is a feeble transmission of her feeling, "I don't know"
Belatedly, I begin to feel sort of sad
the sadness is not of an excruciating kind
I know I parted from people and things dear to me
but the hard lump in me that was painful and tormenting before I
    died
is slowly dissolving now
Is this an end or a beginning?

I smell a lovely aroma. The unforgettable scent
comes right into my heart
Once I had a lover who was a violinist
After we did it she played the violin for me, naked
the fine sinuous tune of her violin and her scent
blended and seeped into my skin

At that time, for no reason, I thought,
I have not only my flesh, but also a soul
Suddenly there is a loud vibration as the boat's screws reverse
    and it comes to a stop.
From somewhere a group of men boisterously comes on board

All of them wear combat fatigues covered with dried mud
some are still holding hand grenades
Suddenly one of them laughingly asks
"Are we dead?
I feel somehow the wind is blowing through me"
saying so they are joking to each other
I feel I have heard their laughter in my mother's womb
Dense fog swirls and the boat clumsily starts again

Strangely I see the boat below me
It fades out, like a movie, as a face fades in
That is my own face, pale, with unkempt whiskers
I would have seen this face in the mirror all the time but I can't
    believe it's my own
I am not sure if I, the one who is seeing, is myself, either
I try to laugh it away, then my face twitches

I certainly know this feeling as if I were watching someone else
though it is actually me
When I was in high school, I decided to kill myself and stood on
    the roof terrace
with one step forward I would be able to erase my being
but could I really erase myself?
I felt like the sidekick in a comic strip, and came down from the roof

I even discussed something like that over drinks
all of us were young then, so death was like a joke
"What of me remains after my body is gone?"
asked Miwa, and Okumura answered, "Consciousness."
Shōji said, "Once the brain is gone, there won't be
    consciousness."
Tei said, "Whatever the case, we'll see when we die."

All of a sudden I get sucked off the deck of the boat,

and I am in pain as if my chest were in a vise
The bright light blinds me. I am on a white hospital bed
"Honey, Honey" my wife is calling again
I want to tell her to leave me alone, but I can't voice it
but I feel awfully at home with her cheap fragrance

I realize that I am breathing
Just a while ago I had no pain anywhere
but now as if the King of Hell were tormenting me
every part of me is screeching
I guess I am back to my body
I am not sure if I am happy or wretched

A faint sound is approaching from a distance
The sound gently undulates along the ridgeline of mountains
and reaches me like a letter from someone
the music flows like water into me in my terrible pain
It seems I often heard it in my childhood
yet this is like hearing it for the very first time

Ah I've done wrong
with no logical connection violent feelings assault me like a tornado
It's not that I remembered I did something wrong to someone
I just feel like begging for forgiveness
I know I won't be able to die unless I ask for forgiveness
I need to find ways to do that, I think to myself

This world and the other world —
does a melody, like an invisible thread, sew them together?
I don't know where I am now
somehow the pain has eased and simple sadness is with me
am I to get to somewhere from here or not?
all I can do is to walk on, trusting music

This Weaving

["This is a fine weaving," says the old man
"This is good. A fine weaving."
His sinewy hands are shaking on his knees
The old man says, looking up
"This is a fine weaving."
His eyes swim in the air.
Nothing is on his lap.
He's been without his eyesight for a long time now
The old man says, in a hoarse voice
not expecting any agreement,
"This is a fine thing."
"Have some tea," says his son
The tent flutters in the wind
They hear children playing outside
"The pattern repeats itself,
it repeats, and it's fine,
forever and ever"
"Yeah, yeah,"
mumbles his son like a short interlude
"Trees repeat themselves
growing leaves, shedding leaves
ripening fruits, dropping fruits"
chants the old man softly
"Men too repeat themselves
Beasts too repeat themselves
They are born, mate and die
the-y are bor–n, ma–te and di——e"
Perhaps it's an ancient song handed down in this region
The melody gives energy to the old man's voice]

"This is the first scene, before the title appears,"
says the young woman, no make-up on her freckled face

236

"Can you carry this poetic style through to the end?"
asks the middle-aged man with a knit cap
He's perched on a drab steel desk
only one monitor is in the bare room
From the window one can see only a sliver of sky between
    buildings
"In Morocco, or in Mongolia?"
The woman is sipping chai she brought in
"I've never been to either place."
Suddenly the man stands up and walks out of the room
the woman moves as if to follow him, but
instead she stands up and opens the window
Along with warm air a butterfly flutters in
The room gains a bit of flair
As the man returns, the woman asks if he's all right
He gives no answer, but he says
"What do you have for breakfast, usually?"
"Most of the time I have herb tea and a brown-rice biscuit . . ."
"You want to live long, don't you?" he says calmly
"Yes, if I can."
The butterfly keeps fluttering over his head.
"I don't think I'd survive location work overseas."
"Anywhere vast, where no one is around. Either a desert or
    grassy field will be fine."
"I'll rely on the words you write. CG will do the rest."
The woman looks at him. She looks away.
She stands up and goes to the window
Looking down at the people passing along the shop-lined street
    below, the woman says,
"'To create a space in one's mind where there is not a single soul'
I saw it in your proposal"
The man feebly gives a wry smile
Piercing gun shots are coming from the editing room next door
I saw it a while ago, remember? The diary

you scribbled in a worn notebook
when you were 21 or so
You snatched it from my hand
and read it out loud, laughing
I still remember that, that one line
'to create a space in one's mind where there is not a single soul'
In one's mind, even one's own self disappears?
Can one do such a thing, I wondered
But since you have been diagnosed with your illness
you seem intent on getting to that place
I am lonely
I am certain I am in your heart
I know that because I have been happy
but, now, you are trying to shut me out
I want to be with you when we die
. . . we've been to a place where absolutely no one else was
    around
Two of us
wasn't that in Nevada?
we stopped our car in the middle of wilderness and had a beer
it was quiet; the frighteningly deep blue sky showed a few vapor
    trails
while we were there for a good two hours, not a single car
    passed by
we had sex in the shade of a gigantic cactus
were you happy with me then?
were you happy being alive in this world?
Have you noticed I've been carrying an iPod recently?
Maybe because I've been teaching piano for so long
I feel I've had enough of piano music
all I listen to is comedians' stories

[There's nothing here
well, the bed, the chair and the toilet are here, but

238

I don't see them; my mind doesn't allow them in
my wife comes here every day
I am happy about that, but once she leaves I am alone
then the nature of time changes
time cannot be measured by a clock
it cannot be marked by a calendar
in pedantic lingo, it is 'Soul's Time'
which has been flowing on like hidden water
through the subterranean time of my days ever since I was born
I have no strength left to press keys
still I want words
I have no energy to vocalize
yet I want words
I have worked with images for over thirty years
in my own way I've read, understood and narrated
in words that are neither scripts nor voices
words that do not fear being contradictory
words that move deeper into ambiguity
all the time fearing that only a blank sheet of paper and silence
may wait for me at the goal I am aiming at
. . . a space where there is not a single soul
a space where even I don't exist
In that empty space I wanted to place
a single egg
an invisible egg
not knowing what it will produce
not knowing if it will ever hatch]

About a year after the Director died
I wrote a stage play using him as protagonist
it has yet to be staged, but
I often dream of it being performed
when the curtain goes up there is nothing on stage
no one is there

according to my script an actor playing the Director appears
he brings out a desk and chair from the wings and starts writing a
    play
then stagehands and the other characters appear
but in my dream the Director never comes on stage
I, as the author, should be worried about it
but feel relieved that he does not appear
to tell you the truth I don't really want to have lines spoken
even though it's odd to say so since I wrote them myself
seeing that nothing is happening after waiting for a long time
the audience begins to stir
at that moment from somewhere a voice is heard
the voice is no longer the actor's
but the Director's own voice
hesitantly, haltingly he speaks
but it is not clear what he is saying
because I know this is all a dream I am not concerned but
I am screaming in my mind, be silent, be silent
I want him to fix his eyes on me in silence
I want him to come closer to me
but dreams are more ephemeral than memories
the Director often said
a drama starts from where no one is and nothing is
I never believed him
but I am beginning to understand him now
he wanted to create with words
something that is there even when there is no one or nothing
    around
something that fills time and space, which to humans may seem
    a simple void

"This is a weaving the nomads in this region used, isn't it?
Doesn't look that old."
"It was for sale at the museum shop."

"What are you going to do with this swathe?"
"I just bought it because it was in a basket of sale items."
The young man ignores the sagging skin on his older lover's
    cheeks
The westerly sunlight glares on the terrace extending into the
    street
"I guess you haven't seen the first movie I wrote the script for?"
"I was in grade-school then."
She doesn't know what to say next, and falls silent
The wine carafe is empty now
While the conversation is halted, words in her mind keep flowing
<I've written stories for many years now
I don't want to make my own life a story
I would rather be scattered fragments
than working with pieces
to make a jig-saw puzzle of my life>
"Is it out on a DVD, your first piece?"
His laughter is carefree as if he reverted to being a grade school
    kid
She does not answer him, instead she points at the carafe with
    her chin
He orders wine as smoothly as he would in his own mother
    tongue
"What is your graduation thesis about?" asks the woman
"Iconography in a society with no written language," he answers
A thought comes to her suddenly:
<Everything has been given to us already, way back
all that's left for us to do is to assign meanings with words>
A phantom of a large beautiful weaving filled her mind
<The weaving the blind old man saw in the tent
was far from being a jig-saw puzzle
the old man said the pattern, endlessly repeating, was fine
no, it was I, in my youth, who had him say that;
the Director filmed that scene in one take using a novice —

even silence is not our creation
so there's no need to look for words there
because this world deserves silence, rather than babbling>
The woman begins to cry silently
Her young lover watches her simply at a loss

☙

CORNELL EAST ASIA SERIES

127 Ann Sung-hi Lee, tr., *Yi Kwang-su and Modern Korean Literature:* Mujŏng
128 Pang Kie-chung & Michael D. Shin, eds., *Landlords, Peasants, & Intellectuals in Modern Korea*
129 Joan R. Piggott, ed., *Capital and Countryside in Japan, 300–1180: Japanese Historians Interpreted in English*
130 Kyoko Selden & Jolisa Gracewood, eds., *Annotated Japanese Literary Gems: Stories by Tawada Yōko, Nakagami Kenji, and Hayashi Kyōko* (Vol. 1)
131 Michael G. Murdock, *Disarming the Allies of Imperialism: The State, Agitation, and Manipulation during China's Nationalist Revolution, 1922–1929*
132 Noel J. Pinnington, *Traces in the Way: Michi and the Writings of Komparu Zenchiku*
133 Kristen Lee Hunter, tr., Charlotte von Verschuer, *Across the Perilous Sea: Japanese Trade with China and Korea from the Seventh to the Sixteenth Centuries*
134 John Timothy Wixted, *A Handbook to Classical Japanese*
135 Kyoko Selden & Jolisa Gracewood, with Lili Selden, eds., *Annotated Japanese Literary Gems: Stories by Natsume Sōseki, Tomioka Taeko, and Inoue Yasushi* (Vol. 2)
136 Yi Tae-Jin, *The Dynamics of Confucianism and Modernization in Korean History*
137 Jennifer Rudolph, *Negotiated Power in Late Imperial China: The Zongli Yamen and the Politics of Reform*
138 Thomas D. Loooser, *Visioning Eternity: Aesthetics, Politics, and History in the Early Modern Noh Theater*
139 Gustav Heldt, *The Pursuit of Harmony: Poetry and Power in Late Heian Japan*
140 Joan R. Piggott & Yoshida Sanae, *Teishinkōki: The Year 939 in the Journal of Regent Fujiwara no Tadahira*
141 Robert Bagley, *Max Loehr and the Study of Chinese Bronzes: Style and Classification in the History of Art*
142 Edwin A. Cranston, *The Secret Island and the Enticing Flame: Worlds of Memory, Discovery, and Loss in Japanese Poetry*
143 Hugh de Ferranti, *The Last Biwa Singer: A Blind Musician in History, Imagination and Performance*
144 Roger Des Forges, Gao Minglu, Liu Chiao-mei, Haun Saussy, with Thomas Burkman, eds., *Chinese Walls in Time and Space: A Multidisciplinary Perspective*
145 George Sidney & Hye-jin Juhn Sidney, trs., *I Heard Life Calling Me: Poems of Yi Sŏng-bok*
146 Sherman Cochran & Paul G. Pickowicz, eds., *China on the Margins*
147 Wang Lingzhen & Mary Ann O'Donnell, trs., *Years of Sadness: Autobiographical Writings of Wang Anyi*
148 John Holstein, tr., *A Moment's Grace: Stories from Korea in Transition*
149 Sunyoung Park with Jefferson J.A. Gatrall, trs., *On the Eve of the Uprising and Other Stories from Colonial Korea*
150 Brother Anthony of Taizé & Lee Hyung-Jin, trs., *Walking on a Washing Line: Poems of Kim Seung-Hee*
151 Matthew Fraleigh, *New Chronicles of Yanagibashi and Diary of A Journey to the West: Narushima Ryūhoku Reports from Home and Abroad*
152 Pei Huang, *Reorienting the Manchus: A Study of Sinicization, 1583–1795*
153 Karen Gernant & Chen Zeping, trs., *White Poppies and Other Stories by Zhang Kangkang*
154 Marina Svensson & Mattias Burrell, eds., *Making Law Work: Chinese Laws in Context*
155 Tomoko Aoyama & Barbara Hartley, trs., *Indian Summer by Kanai Mieko*
156 Lynne Kutsukake, tr., *Single Sickness and Other Stories by Masuda Mizuko*
157 Takako Lento, tr., *Tanikawa Shuntarō: The Art of Being Alone, Poems 1952–2009*
158 Shu-ning Sciban & Fred Edwards, eds., *Endless War: Fiction and Essays by Wang Wen-hsing*
159 Elizabeth Oyler & Michael Watson, eds., *Like Clouds or Mists: Studies and Translations of Nō Plays of the Genpei War*
160 Michiko N. Wilson & Michael K. Wilson, trs., *Minako Ōba: Of Birds Crying*

9 781933 947570